THE BEST PLAYS FROM THE STRAWBERRY ONE-ACT FESTIVAL

Volume Seven

Compiled by Van Dirk Fisher

iUniverse, Inc.
Bloomington

The Best Plays From The Strawberry One-Act Festival
Volume Seven

iUniverse books may be ordered through booksellers or by contacting:

iUniverse
1663 Liberty Drive
Bloomington, IN 47403
www.iuniverse.com
1-800-Authors (1-800-288-4677)

ISBN: 978-1-4759-8729-4 (sc)
ISBN: 978-1-4759-8730-0 (e)

Printed in the United States of America

iUniverse rev. date: 4/24/2013

Welcome to the 7th Volume of the Best Plays From The Strawberry One-Act Festival. The Strawberry One-Act Festival, which began in 1995 in New York City, is the brainchild of The Riant Theatre's Artistic Director, Van Dirk Fisher. The festival is a play competition in which the audience and the theatre's judges cast their votes to select the best play of the season.

Twice a year, hundreds of plays from across the country are submitted for the competition, of which 40 are chosen to compete. Plays move from the 1st round to the semi-finals and then the finals. The playwright of the winning play receives a grant and the opportunity to have a full-length play developed by the Riant. In addition, awards are given out for Best Director, Best Actor and Best Actress.

This anthology includes plays from the Summer of 2009 through the Winter of 2011. The Strawberry One-Act Festival is a wonderful opportunity for the audience and the industry alike to see some of the best talent in the nation. Every performance features three to four dynamic one-act plays. There's always a lot of buzz surrounding each performance as artists converge and network on future projects. Several of the playwrights whose plays are featured in the festival have written for the literary world, as well as for television and film. "We are very fortunate to be able to fulfill our mission, which is to discover and develop talent and playwrights for the stage," says Mr. Fisher. "We are very proud of this accomplishment, but the work doesn't stop there. Competition aside, everyone's a winner in the festival, because several actors, directors and playwrights are chosen to work on future projects at the Riant."

During the Summer 2010 Festival, the audience's votes – as well as those of the playwrights in attendance -- selected SOMETHING LIKE PENGUINS by Levi Wilson as the Best Play of the Season. The winner of the Winter 2011 Festival was BRYAN AND KIM by Adam Delia.

The first play in this anthology is SOMETHING LIKE PENGUINS by Levi Wilson, a delightful romantic comedy about a young man who returns home months early from a volunteer crusade abroad only to find out that his best friend and his fiancé are now living together. I love this play it was definitely a crowd pleaser.

All is fair in love, but when it comes to matters of the heart and marriage it can be a slippery slope when one spouse suspects the other of infidelity. Kristen Seavey's play THE LOSING GAME is a bitter sweet romantic drama about Rue, a florist, who's seeking companionship from a co-worker, because she believes her husband Simon, a psychiatrist, is having an affair. Communication is so important in relationships and so is trust. This well crafted drama is full of surprises and passion.

What would you do for love? Would you be willing to go to couple's therapy if your girlfriend was battling with a secret so dark that it was debilitating and preventing her from having sex? Well that's exactly what Bryan decides to do in Adam Delia's award winning play BRYAN AND KIM. This play shook me to my very core. The dynamics of love and challenges this couple faces is a true testament to unconditional love.

Going through growing pains in High School and College is hard enough, but having your sexuality being questioned repeatedly can be frustrating. LOVE FOR BEGINNERS by Cesar Abella is a tender coming of age story about a young man named Noah, who's in love with a girl named Hallie, but she refuses to take him seriously because she thinks he's gay. It goes so far as to make him actually question his sexuality, but in the end all that really matters is that he learns to be true to himself and not allow people to place him in a box with labels.

When the love of our life dies can we ever find true love again? IT'S GREEK TO ME by Shelley Bromberg, a romantic comedy, tackles this dilemma. After 25 years of marriage to her wonderful husband, Solomon, Selma visits his gravesite at the unveiling of his tombstone. Their children have purchased a single ticket for her to take a trip to Greece, a place that Solomon and her wanted to go to before he died, but first she wants a sign from him to let her know it's okay to go without him. And low and behold when she opens the envelope to look at the ticket it's from Solomon Tours. So away she goes to Greece, where she meets Mikos, a beautiful Greek masseuse, who captures her heart and gives her a private tour of the island. But can she allow herself to fall in love again without feeling guilty? That's the challenge she's faced with now, and it's a journey that's exciting and full of humor fit for the young at heart.

On the other side of the spectrum is MI MEDIA NARANJA by Rolls Andre, a raunchy comedy about a married couple whose decision to have a threesome puts their lives in a precarious situation when their invited guest, a woman, ends up dying during their tryst. The play begins with them franticly trying to decide what to do with the body, which they left in the bathtub. This play pushes all the right buttons as this couple discovers just how far they are willing to go to save their marriage and themselves.

The next play BIRD WATCHING by Jeffrey L. Hollman is a very clever play about a man and woman who are in Central Park after having a little afternoon delight at a nearby hotel. The married woman, who is visiting from out of town, is very much in love with the man, but it seems that because of their present situation there are limitations and all they can have now are these little stolen moments. This day unbeknownst to both of them will be very different, because of a young man who is also in the park doing a little… Bird Watching. This play is very juicy. I'll leave you to read it for yourself to savor every morsel.

Family secrets are very painful when they are exposed and that's probably why no one dares to talk about it. The truth can be too much to bear. E.K. Deutsch's play TURKEY DAY, mixes the perfect blend of human angst with a dysfunctional family that stirs up raw emotion that one can only expect when the family gathers for Thanksgiving dinner. Actress Tamar Pelzig won the Best Actress Award for her portrayal of the role of Poo, a young troubled teenage daughter.

A troubled mind like the death of a loved one can be too much to tolerate. Dr. Renee Baylor, a psychiatrist in Ellen Orchid's play PERSCRIPTIONS discovers the painful truth of this matter when she decides to allow her patient Anita, to house sit for her while she attends a conference out of town. But their relationship takes a dramatic turn when Anita comes over to learn the rules of the house. This play has so many layers and depth to its characters. It's a good play for actresses with great skill and talent.

Sometimes the visible scars in life are harder to overcome than the emotional scars that are hidden from our eyes. But the heart sees what it wants to see. It feels what it wants to feel and fights for what it needs in order to live like the very air we breathe. FIREMAN by Stephen Brown is an advocate of this belief and proves it wonderfully in his play about a fireman whose face has been severely scarred by a fire and his lover who can only see the beautiful man that he loves.

HEROES by Joseph Lizardi, is a powerful play and a tribute to our veterans, who are often forgotten and not well provided for when they return from war. Our hero, Jeffrey Lewis, a Vietnam veteran, Afro-American, with a badly damaged left leg, who is desperate, prone to violence, and suffering from Post Vietnam Syndrome, is on a job interview with Steve Gailey, an arrogant, self absorbed and indifferent man. Jeffrey is at his wits end trying for one last time to get a job so he can support himself and his wife and hold his head up like a man. Colin Knight won the Best Actor Award for his portrayal of Jeffrey and managed to bring empathy to his character that even the harden

Mr. Gailey was even moved to show compassion in the end. But is it a little too late and not enough to erase the spoils of war? Find out in this thought provoking drama about our heroes.

The last play in this anthology is the comedy COMPUBOTS by Paul Trupia, about a husband who buys a set of adult size male and female robots for his wife and himself. It's a very funny comedy, where these computer robots can do everything from receive phone messages, recommend restaurants, cultural events, clothing sales, investment tips and even balance your checking account. Like a loyal companion and friend, this happily married couple, learn a painful lesson a little too late from putting too much trust and information into technology.

I hope that you enjoy these plays as much as I have with the hundreds of people who have seen them in the Strawberry One-Act Festival. Share them with your friends and family. If they make you laugh or cry, entertain you or even enlighten you in any way, then I guess they have served their purpose: to touch people's souls.

Enjoy them and if you're ever in New York City during the months of February or August, be sure to check out the Strawberry One-Act Festival. We've also added full-length plays as part of the Strawberry Theatre Festival, both festivals run during the same time. In addition, you can check out The Video Diaries Project: A Series of Short Films about the Artists in the Strawberry One-Act Festival. You can view the short films for free on our website www.therianttheatre.com as well as see the other plays and workshops we produce. You may also follow us on Twitter at www.twitter.com/RiantTheatre and on Facebook at www.facebook.com/RiantTheatre. And know that at the Riant Theatre you are always welcome, welcome, WELCOME!

Van Dirk Fisher
Founder & Artistic Director
The Riant Theatre
P.O. Box 1902
New York, NY 10013
RiantTheatre@gmail.com

To hear some great music go to www.cdbaby.com/cd/toejambeats or www.myspace.com/toejambeats419 or www.myspace.com/lovingyouthemusical

CONTENTS

Ryan Lee Nazionale *as ELI*, Janaya Combs *as HEATHER*,
Levi Wilson *as DANIEL*
in SOMETHING LIKE PENGUINS by Levi Wilson.

SOMETHING LIKE PENGUINS

By Levi Wilson

Levi Wilson is a BA Graduate of the University of Kentucky's Theatre Arts Department and has studied at the Beverly Hills Playhouse in Los Angeles and The Stella Adler Studio of Acting. He has written and appeared in several film festival Official Selection shorts and the CMJ Film Festival Best Feature *The Invisible Life of Thomas*. He is an avid martial artist. This is his first play.

Something Like Penguins made its New York City debut on August 15, 2010 at the Theater at St. Clements for the Riant Theatre's Summer 2010 Strawberry One-Act Festival where it won Best Play with the following cast, in order of appearance:

ELI	Ryan Lee Nazionale
DANIEL	Levi Wilson
HEATHER	Janaya Combs

The play was directed by Mario Corry.

CAST OF CHARACTERS
ELI, a volunteer, is in his twenties. He is tired from a long journey.
DANIEL, Daniel's best friend, is in his twenties.
HEATHER, Daniel's fiancée, is in her twenties. She is spritely, earnest and open.

NOTE FROM THE AUTHOR

This play is meant to be performed casually and off the cuff. The actors are encouraged to improvise around the scripted lines and overlap each other.

The actors should be free to make exasperated and vaulted exclamations suitable to the heightened emotions of the situation. Though not specified, the *ringtone* sound cue ought to be as obnoxious a song as possible and hint at the relationship between Heather and Daniel. This is a special ringtone Daniel has for Heather.

SCENE I
(A stoop in New York City. It is early morning. The sun is shining. The birds are chirping. After a moment a young man walks onto the stage. This is ELI. He is slightly disheveled, perhaps a lot of facial hair, as if he has been traveling for some time and from some distance. He could use some sleep. His dress is very casual, worn jeans, worn combat boots, perhaps a weathered North Face jacket, and a full hiker's backpack. He stops at the stoop and breaths a heavy sigh. He reaches in his pocket for the keys but they are not there. He unshoulders his backpack and digs in its pockets for a moment. As he digs another young man enters from the opposite side of the stage. He is lightly disheveled but in a different way. He isn't tired but has a light step, almost dancing, as he walks toward the stoop. This is DANIEL. He is wearing a wrinkled buttoned dress shirt, tucked, and slacks and dress shoes with no socks. In one arm is a small brown bag of sundry groceries and in the other hand is a carefully balanced cardboard travel tray with two coffees on them. DANIEL takes a few steps towards the stoop and spots Eli. He stops.)
    ELI: Dammit!
(By this time the backpack is half empty with pieces of clothing and travel items placed on the stoop. He pulls out a small item carefully wrapped with ribbon and bow and places that carefully on the stoop. DANIEL is frozen like a gazelle listening for a lion. ELI looks up after placing the present and stops DANIEL.)
    ELI: Daniel!
    DAN: Eli! Whatever?
    ELI: Yeah, man! It's me!
    DAN: I can see that!
    ELI: I'm back, man!
    DAN: You made it back alive.
    ELI: Who's gonna stop me?
    DAN: Nobody, apparently!
    ELI: Put that shit down and give me a hug, man!
    DAN: Okay!
    (DANIEL walks to the stoop and puts everything down. They embrace like brothers, veterans of an ancient war.)
    ELI: Good to see you. Can't find my keys.
    DAN: That sucks.
    ELI: You know you leave home for a while and you don't use your keys.

Sometimes they just kind of disappear, like if you don't believe in it enough it just fades away.

DAN: Maybe if you clap your hands they'll come back.

ELI: Right!

(DAN and ELI close their eyes and bring their hands together with one definitive clap!)

DAN and ELI: Hear me, God of Keys!

(ELI starts to rifle and dig in his backpack again. Dan takes a seat on the stoop. He takes a sip of one of the coffees. He looks up at the apartment. Then back at ELI.)

DAN: Wow. I can't believe you're already back.

ELI: Tell me about it! I thought I'd be gone for—

DAN: Ten months—

ELI: Ten months. What's new with you?

DAN: New? Oh, god. Nothing really. Nothing really going on. Not right now, anyways.

ELI: No?

DAN: Nope. I mean, I've got some things lined up, you know. For the future–for in the–later on.

ELI: Oh. That's cool. Seeing anyone?

DAN: Not yet. Not right now really.

ELI: Really? That's it, man. I'm making it my mission to find you a girl. You have been single too long. You have got to be tired of being a third wheel with me and Heather? Right, man?

DAN: The thought had crossed my mind.

ELI: Now that I'm back Heather and I can speed up her move-in and then the game is afoot!

DAN: You know, it's not something I'm worried about. I'm more interested in my work.

ELI: Work? You just said you had nothing going on? Come on!

DAN: I've got things. Lined up—

ELI: Yeah, yeah. Lined up for later on. In the 'future.'

DAN: That's the one.

(Pause)

ELI: Did you move?

DAN: No. Why?

ELI: Well, it's kind of a trek from East 90th for a coffee.

DAN: Oh, yeah. Yeah, I mean, you're telling me!

(ELI feels something in his backpack.)

ELI: Oh, I think I've got it!

(He reaches and pulls out a ring of Allen wrenches.)

3

ELI: Shit!

(*ELI take is backpack and flips it upside down and dumps the contents onto the sidewalk. The rest of his stuff is now lying on the ground. He flings the contents about, digs, feels around for anything resembling keys. It is a futile effort. The keys are gone.*)

ELI: I guess I should have clapped more. I guess I was gone too long this time.

DAN: Yeah.

(*Pause*)

DAN: So, then. What now?

ELI: What now what?

DAN: What's the next step?

ELI: I have to get a job, man, I guess.

DAN: I mean now…

ELI: Now? This second. You wanna get some breakfast with me?

DAN: You know, I've got to get back up.

ELI: Get back up? I just got back and you've got to go?

DAN: I do. I've got to make a phone call. Take a shower.

ELI: Daniel. Hey, your coffees and stuff!

DAN: Right!

ELI: Let's go get some breakfast somewhere. I need to brainstorm.

(*DANIEL picks up his bag and the coffee tray.*)

DAN: Look, I got this–I'm not really hungry, let's just meet up a little later. I need to shower—

ELI: You don't have to eat anything. I just have to sit somewhere and–I got it! Duh!

DAN: You got it?

ELI: Break into my apartment.

DAN: What?

ELI: Help me break in!

(*A ringing noise. It is DANIEL's cell phone.*)

ELI: That is an obnoxious ringtone.

DAN: Yeah. Yeah.

(*DANIEL does nothing. The phone rings.*)

ELI: You gonna get it?

DAN: Right! Right.

(*DANIEL puts his stuff down again and fumbles for his phone. He finds it. It stops ringing.*)

DAN: Missed it.

ELI: Was that the call you gotta make?

DAN: Huh? Oh. Uh, yeah, no. Call blocked. You know.

ELI: Creditors.

DAN: Creditors.

(Pause. DANIEL slowly gathers his things.)

ELI: Okay. So help me break into my apartment.

DAN: Oh, god. You know. I really gotta get going.

ELI: Come on, man! We've done this before!

DAN: Jeez, I mean. I'm, I need—

ELI: Man, second floor! I just need to quick boost.

DAN: I know—

ELI: I got a spare set in my desk. Just a quick boost, I'm in, you can take your shower and we can meet up.

DAN: Look. Hey, okay? The coffee is getting cold, the croissants are getting stale. I can't be here.

ELI: Okay.

DAN: Okay?

ELI: Okay.

DAN: Okay, then.

(DANIEL turns slowly on his heels.)

ELI: What the fuck is going on? I haven't seen you in months! You have some important engagement to get to? You're in such a rush you have to go 70 blocks for two coffees and a bag of croissants?! You have somebody tied up in your apartment? You know, man! Go home. I'll break into the apartment myself.

DAN: Look. Okay, wait. Okay. I'm sorry.

ELI: So, you'll help me back in my apartment?

DAN: Let's just, how about we go to the diner down there and have some breakfast?

ELI: You want to have breakfast now?

DAN: Let's have some breakfast.

ELI: I'm sorry, man. I'm just fucking tired, you know? I'm been on three different planes traveling half-way around the world. I'm so frustrated, our funding got cut! That's why I'm back early. I wanted to let everyone know but our satellite phone got damaged a couple weeks ago. So, I couldn't call Heather, I couldn't call my parents. It's been one thing after another. And now I can't find my keys.

DAN: Yeah.

ELI: You know, man. I'm not even hungry. You should take a shower. I'm gotta repack all of this and find a way in. Shouldn't be too hard.

DAN: Okay!

(ELI starts to repack his stuff. He seems defeated. DANIEL stands a few feet away, watching. He slowly turns to walk away.)

ELI: I really wanted to do some good in the world, man. You know? I can't even get that right. We didn't run out of funding, man. They kicked me out. I collapsed three tents. It destroyed a lot of equipment including the satellite transmitter. I didn't lose my satellite phone. I never even had one. So they sent me home.

(Silence)

DAN: Is there anything I can do?

ELI: You could help me break into my place.

DAN: Uh…

ELI: I know, man. I'm kidding. I just don't see how it could get any worse.

(The door at the top of the stoop flies open. A girl appears. This is Heather. Her hair is in a quick and messy ponytail. She is wearing only a bathrobe. She stands outside and spots DANIEL first.)

HEATHER: Hey! I thought you got hit by a car—

DAN: Heather!

ELI: Heather? Oh, man, my luck is finally turning!

(Heather screeches as she sees ELI get up and walk up the stairs towards her.)

ELI: It's really me! I'm back. Oh, man, did I miss you!

(He embraces Heather. She reciprocates after the initial shock.)

HEATHER: You're back. You're really here!

ELI: I had such a shitty time. I'm done with volunteering! I just can't be away from you that long.

HEATHER: Oh, god! You're here!

ELI: I don't think I really realized how done I was until I saw you!

HEATHER: So, you're really back. For good?

ELI: Yeah.

(He gives her a long kiss. Heather relaxes into it and kisses back. DANIEL clears his throat loudly. They don't notice. He coughs slightly louder. They still don't notice. He tosses his coffees to the ground with a loud cough.)

ELI: Shit! Oh, man! My best friend, my fiancée. I'm starving! Let's get some breakfast. Man, you spilled your coffee!

DAN: Let's have some breakfast. What about your keys?

ELI: Right on!

(ELI runs upstairs and disappears behind the door. Heather is mortified.)

HEATHER: What are you doing?

DAN: What?

HEATHER: Why did you send him up for the keys?

DAN: Did I do that?

HEATHER: Yes!

DAN: I did do that.

HEATHER: Why did you do that?

DAN: What are you going to tell him?

HEATHER: Tell him? I don't know. He's back.

DAN: I know he's back. Are you going to tell him—? What's been going on?

HEATHER: I—

DAN: Well, you have to, right? You're in love, right? We're in love.

HEATHER: I—

DAN: Heather, I love you.

HEATHER: I—

DAN: Heather!

HEATHER: Daniel. No, I love you. I love you so much!

DAN: I love you, too. So, what are we doing?

HEATHER: Is that why you sent him up?

DAN: He's got to know sooner or later.

HEATHER: Later!

DAN: Later?

HEATHER: Yes!

DAN: He's back now, so that's it.

HEATHER: No.

DAN: Wait. So, you are choosing him over me.

HEATHER: No!

DAN: No? What do you mean 'no?' So he's back early, but that doesn't change what has to happen.

HEATHER: Oh, God.

DAN: Oh, God.

HEATHER: I am not prepared for this.

DAN: Not prepared? What? I—

HEATHER: I don't want to deal with this! I can't break up with him! I love him!

DAN: What the fuck are you talking about? You love him? Everything you said to me? He was gone all the time. Still trying to find himself. Looking all over the world. He's too selfish to have a real relationship with you. Ring a bell?

HEATHER: And he's a good person!

DAN: Are you trying to make me crazy? We have to tell him. I know you wanted to wait but he's back now, early. The timing sucks but that's how it's got to be.

HEATHER: No! I don't know!

DAN: Yes.

HEATHER: No.

DAN: Yes!

HEATHER: No!

DAN: *Yes!*

HEATHER: Wait. No! Does he even have to know?

DAN: Kinda!

(Heather closes the distance between them. She gently kisses him. DANIEL does not move. He pulls keys out of his pocket, ELI's spare keys, and jingles them in front of her.)

HEATHER: Daniel—

(ELI steps out of the door. He is disturbed. He stands at the stop of the stoop. Heather quickly snatches the keys from DANIEL.)

ELI: I couldn't find my keys.

(Heather holds the keys up and jingles them.)

ELI: Oh. Good.

(ELI angrily walks down the stairs and receives the keys.)

ELI: Now I can get into my house. Place. Apartment. Daniel. You aren't wearing any socks.

DAN: No.

ELI: Or a belt.

DAN: Yeah.

ELI: There's a jacket up there. Looks like it might go well with those pants.

HEATHER: Eli.

ELI: Fuck you. Fuck you both.

HEATHER: Eli. Don't. Oh, god, what do I do? Eli. Eli?

(ELI fumbles through his backpack. The others can't see that he finds a small pocket knife. He unfolds it.)

DAN: Look, Eli. Uhm.

ELI: Fuck you, man!

(ELI lunges at DANIEL with the knife. With quick, deft movements DANIEL disarms ELI, locks his arm, and easily places him on the ground. DANIEL is above him, ELI is completely prostrate.)

DAN: I don't want to fight you. We can talk this out.

ELI: Let me up.

DAN: Okay.

(DANIEL releases him.)

ELI: I don't want to talk this out.

(ELI lunges for DANIEL again, fists flying. DANIEL calmly dodges the punches and lands one of his own squarely in ELI's chest. ELI stops cold, he stumbles bad grabbing his chest. He coughs and collapses to the ground.)

ELI: *Fuck.*

DAN: Shit.

HEATHER: Eli.

(Heather runs down to ELI and comforts him. He makes some minor effort to shove her away to no avail.)

HEATHER: Why did you have to do that?

DAN: I wasn't going to let him stab me.

HEATHER: He would have gotten off. It was a crime of passion.

DAN: That would have made me feel a lot better.

(Heather stands and gestures for DANIEL to help ELI. DANIEL walks to ELI and holds out a hand.)

DAN: Come on.

ELI: Oh, fuck you, man. I don't need a hand up from you.

DAN: It's the least I can do.

ELI: I'm sure you could do less.

DAN: You're my best friend, okay! I still care about you. Let me help you up.

ELI: No! I'm not letting you help me up. I don't even want to get up now. I like it down here. It can't get any worse down here.

HEATHER: Stop it! Stop fighting!

DAN: Who's fighting? I'm trying to be nice.

HEATHER: I want us to be friends again.

ELI: You don't get to help me up, either.

HEATHER: No! Eli. Let's be friends!

DAN: We're friends. Everything is fine.

ELI: No, everything is not fine. I don't know if you're my friends. Who are you people?

HEATHER: Daniel—

ELI: That's right. Go on! I'm fine right here.

HEATHER: Daniel! Help me! Help me fix this!

DAN: What the hell! You love him. You fix it.

HEATHER: I don't want this! I want it back to how it was!

ELI: Wait a second, man. How long has this been going on? How long has there been this thing between the you two and the me out of town?

DAN: Three years. Just three years.

ELI: Three years! Jesus Fucking Christ, three years? I thought we had something. I thought it was special.

HEATHER: We do, Eli! I love you!

DAN: She told me that, too!

ELI: You told him! How could you tell him it was special? Did you tell him it was special?

DAN: Five minutes ago!

ELI: How can it be special with two guys? You can't! You can't have special with two guys. It's the math. It's fuzzy math! Special plus two equals no!

DAN: It's biologically impossible!

HEATHER: I don't care if it biologically impossible!

ELI: You got too much love.

HEATHER: Isn't that a good thing? Isn't that what we want?

DAN: Not in this case!

HEATHER: Daniel. I love you because you are intelligent, surprising, spontaneous, and you can beat up a guy without breaking a sweat.

ELI: Thank you.

HEATHER: Eli. I love you because you are kind and gentle and sensitive and always trying to be a better person.

ELI: I am.

DAN: How is that supposed to help us? That doesn't help us at all!

ELI: Wait a second! Speak for yourself, I was feeling good there for a second.

DAN: You're an idiot?

HEATHER: I'm giving him love and I'm giving you love.

ELI: Yeah, it's more love.

DAN: Oh, more love. Okay, you can be the second husband!

HEATHER: Penguins!

DAN: Penguins?

HEATHER: Penguins take a new mate every year. I watched it on one of your stupid documentaries.

ELI: You guys watch documentaries together?

DAN: What do you do?

ELI: We—

HEATHER: *We* don't do anything. *He* goes off to save the world.

ELI: I saw one of those ads where you can save the children for a few pennies a day—

HEATHER: Penguins! A new mate every year.

DAN: Yes! But one at a time. Not at the same time!

ELI: And I'm not a penguin.

DAN: Were you even paying attention to this documentary?

HEATHER: I don't care about documentaries and I hate fucking penguins!

DAN: You brought it up!

HEATHER: I know!

(ELI collapses to the ground again, exasperated.)

HEATHER: Come on! Stand up! Be a man about this!

DAN: He's not even a man.

ELI: I'm a man. It works. Tell him it works.

HEATHER: How should I know? You haven't been here in a while.

DAN: And who's picking up the slack?

HEATHER: If you weren't gone all of the time maybe this wouldn't have happened!

DAN: That's right!

HEATHER: Wait. Shut up!

DAN: Oh, I thought we were, it was his fault—

HEATHER: Shut up! I love you both! I love you both! You! Dan. You are just too smart for your own good! I love your brains. But you won't ever open up to me! We can't talk about anything deep, anything important! And I'm sick of watching documentaries.

DAN: Okay. I guess we can change the Netflix queue. What do you want to watch?

HEATHER: *Clueless.*

DAN: *Clueless* sucks.

ELI: *I* like *Clueless.*

HEATHER: And you! I wish you would stop running away from all of your problems! When are you going to stop crusading around the world and solve your own problems? I wish you would stand up for yourself sometime! Stop dumping all of the world's troubles on your head.

ELI: You're right. I'm such an asshole.

HEATHER: Listen to yourselves! Why can't you be one man? That's what I want. I want all the good things from you and all the good things from you, put them into one man, and throw the rest away. Why can't I combine you into one perfect man?

(Pause)

ELI: Because *that* would be biologically impossible.

DAN: I think with current genetic technologies—

(Heather screams in frustration. She sinks down to the bottom of the stairs and cries. She wails. She cries for an uncomfortable amount of time. DANIEL and ELI run to her sides to comfort her. Heather eventually recovers herself. She sniffles a bit, wipes her face off. She smiles cutely.)

HEATHER: Can we get some breakfast?

(Pause.)

DAN: Sure.

ELI: Kay.

(Lights fade to Black.)
(The End)

THE LOSING GAME

By Kristen Seavey

Kristen Seavey is a 2010 graduate of the American Musical and Dramatic Academy in New York City. Originally from Maine, her plays have been produced in various locations around the state. A working actor and performer, *The Losing Game* marks her New York debut as a writer.

The Losing Game made its New York City debut on August 15th, 2010 at the St. Clement's Theatre. It was a semi-finalist in The Riant Theatre's Summer 2010 Strawberry One-Act Festival with the following cast, in order of appearance:

TODD	Joseph Boover
RUE	Kristen Seavey
SIMON	Bryant Martin
LUCY	Meg Zrini

The play was directed by Cate Smit and Jim Elliott, and stage managed by Patricia Mason.

CAST OF CHARACTERS

TODD, a charming and nerdy florist in mid twenties.
RUE, a florist in her mid twenties seeking companionship.
SIMON, a psychiatrist in his late twenties, dedicated to his job.
LUCY, a woman in her early twenties seeking professional help.

(Lights up inside a flower shop. RUE, a pretty woman about mid twenties, and

TODD, *a slightly nerdy but charming man also mid twenties are working. RUE is working on an arrangement, and TODD is singing and humming "You Are So Beautiful To Me" while tending a rose very gingerly.)*

RUE: Todd, you are such a weirdo.

TODD: What?

RUE: You know what…

TODD: It's stuck in my head! *(He begins singing poorly again and dancing with the rose.)*

RUE: Todd, stop! You look ridiculous. I need your help with this.

TODD: So what if I do. Nobody's in here.

RUE: Okay. Mrs. Vasquez. Her goldfish died. I need something that's not cliché.

TODD: Somebody ordered an arrangement for her goldfish?

RUE: "Sorry for your loss."

TODD: When was the last time you went out dancing? I can't remember the last time I went.

RUE: I can tell.

TODD: Hey! What I just did was great.

RUE: That's because impossible to step on a rose's foot.

TODD: Okay, okay.

RUE: Simon doesn't like dancing.

TODD: Simon… I don't understand that guy.

(Lights out. Lights come up on a kitchen. It is morning. SIMON, a professional looking man in his late twenties is sitting at the table reading a paper. RUE enters after a beat.)

SIMON: Morning. You look lovely. *(He goes to kiss her, but her acceptance isn't friendly.)* What's the matter?

RUE: Where were you last night?

SIMON: Ruthie! I'm sorry. I got held up at the office. Last minute meeting. You know how it is.

RUE: Sure, I know how it is…

SIMON: Don't give me that! We've just been busy lately. There are more clients coming in now than I've ever seen.

RUE: That's what you always tell me. You're busy; you got tied up … new appointment.

SIMON: I know, I know, and I'm sorry. I shouldn't have done that to you.

RUE: And is this the part where I'm supposed to believe you?

SIMON: Oh come on. Ruthie you're killing me. I'll make it up to you. You know I love you.

RUE: *(Smiling.)* I know…

SIMON: I'll take you out to dinner sometime, a night on the town. Just the two of us.

RUE: *(Grinning.)* I think you owe me a lot more than that.

SIMON: Do I? *(She nods and they kiss.)* I'll call you later, alright?

RUE: Okay. Have a good day at work.

SIMON: You too. Say hello to the flowers for me.

RUE: I will.

(SIMON winks at her and RUE smiles, watching him as he exits. Lights fade.)

(Lights up in the flower shop with RUE and TODD in mid-conversation while doing misc. work.)

RUE: I shouldn't have even told you…

TODD: You shouldn't have to eat alone practically every night, Rue.

RUE: You do it.

TODD: Yes, but that's different.

RUE: He's really not as bad as I'm making you think he is. The man has just been unbelievably busy lately.

TODD: *Unbelievably* I think is the key word there…

RUE: What?

TODD: You really believe that he's at *work* all of those nights? I mean, does that really happen?

RUE: What are you trying to say?

TODD: Are you sure he's only seeing his clients?

RUE: Todd! That's an awful thing to say. You don't even know him. Simon is a very honest man… Don't be so stupid. *(Flings a flower at him. He flings a flower back.)* Hey!

TODD: You started it.

(He tosses flowers at her. In an effort to avoid them, she knocks over the bucket of roses on the counter. They scatter in a mess.)

RUE: Todd!

TODD: Sorry, Rue.

(He begins cleaning them up off the floor and handing them to her one at a time, speeding up faster than she can put them into the bucket - Ad-libbing on each rose.)

She thinks I'm funny, she thinks I'm funny not, she thinks I'm funny, she likes my glasses, she wants to kill me… *(etc… On the last rose)* Annnnd I'm gonna have to keep this one. Sorry.

(They laugh and lights fade.)

(Lights up on the inside of a therapist's office. SIMON sits in a chair with a few papers spread out on his lap and a clipboard, taking occasional notes. LUCY

sits on a couch. Very subtly, she rubs her fingers and nails across her wrist, as if making a cutting motion. It should seem almost subconscious. Their relationship is strictly professional.)

LUCY: Sometimes I just wish he wouldn't have left me, but I know he deserved better than what I was giving him. *(Pause)* I just wish I could to talk to him again...

SIMON: Well you know you can't change the past Lucy, all you can do is make the best of it.

LUCY: It's just hard to live with the fact that when I had the chance to talk to him, I didn't.

SIMON: A relationship is give and take.

LUCY: Good thing I know that now...

SIMON: You are not responsible for the bad things that happen to you.

LUCY: I know...

SIMON: Accidents happen. You still loved him, and he knew that. Correct?

LUCY: ...Yes, he did. And I'm glad he did. I wish I could tell him once more though...

SIMON: Death is a hard thing to cope with, Lucy... Especially when it's somebody you care about.

LUCY: *(Pause)* I do a lot of wishful thinking...

SIMON: It's your escape.

LUCY: It doesn't really do much for me.

SIMON: We're just at about time, but I want you to keep journaling... It's going to benefit you very much, I promise. *(He notices her hand movement. She stops and their eyes meet. Pause.)* Can I pencil you in for an extra session this week? My schedule is open for any time as of right now.

LUCY: I'm fine with anything after 5.

SIMON: Alright then, how about Thursday. At 6:30?

LUCY: Thursday it is.

SIMON: Excellent.

(Lights out.)

(Lights up on RUE inside the flower shop. She is working on an arrangement. TODD is watering the flowers around the shop.)

RUE: He told me last night that the therapist next door to him quit. So the office has happily booked almost half of his old clients with Simon...

TODD: Is that bad?

RUE: I should be proud of him.

TODD: You are proud of him.

RUE: No, I'm just selfish. He deserves somebody who will support him...

TODD: No, *you* deserve somebody who will appreciate you.

RUE: He does appreciate me...

TODD: Does he?

(SIMON unexpectedly enters the shop.)

RUE: *(Surprised)* Simon! What are you doing here? *(SIMON goes over and kisses her.)*

SIMON: I stopped by to see you.

TODD: I'm surprised you're not working.

SIMON: I'm sorry... Shouldn't you be out back somewhere picking daffodils and tulips?

TODD: Alright... well uh *Rue*, I'm gonna go take care of... the last Teleflora order and put the new shipments in the cooler.

RUE: Okay, thank you Todd. *(TODD exits.)* You know it was unnecessary to speak to him like that...

SIMON: I don't have a lot of time. I'm on my lunch break.

RUE: That's no excuse, Simon. Why are you patronizing my co-worker?

SIMON: Oh for God sakes, Rue. You're being ridiculous.

RUE: No, I'm not. That was completely uncalled for.

SIMON: You're right. I'm sorry — Rue, listen, I'm going to be late tonight. I wouldn't have booked it if I hadn't thought she needed it. Believe me. I'm stressed out enough as it is.

RUE: You expect me to be sympathetic to you?

SIMON: No, but I'm expecting a little understanding...

RUE: Simon, where are your priorities?

SIMON: Ruth, don't do this to me right now.

RUE: What about me?

SIMON: You are being incredibly selfish.

RUE: What. About. Me.

SIMON: Would you listen to yourself? You're telling me to stop patronizing your coworker, and here you are condescending my work. I have people's emotional sanity depending on me every day. It's my responsibility to take care of them when they need me and it comes with sacrifice. Sacrifice that isn't easy for me, Rue. So back off a bit. Please. I'm sorry... I actually came here cause I wanted to give you this... *(Simon pulls out a small box of chocolates.)* I felt bad about having to work late again tonight... I thought maybe this would help...I guess it doesn't do much now... but anyway, here *(She doesn't accept it so he puts it on the counter.)* Well, I've got to be getting back... *(He gathers himself and walks out. RUE stands there for a moment, and TODD enters walking on eggshells. He goes over to the workbench and creates work for himself to avoid talking. RUE watches him for a beat.)*

RUE: Would you... want to get dinner?

(Lights out.)

(Lights up to the sound of LUCY'S voice at a therapy session. SIMON sits in a chair few papers spread out on his lap with a clipboard, taking occasional notes. LUCY now has white bandages wrapped around her wrists, and scratches on her arms. She has a journal in her hands, and is reading from it.)

LUCY: ..." I couldn't understand what he was saying. Then he melted into the ground, and flowers grew in the exact shadow where he was sitting. They were daisies, hundreds of tiny daisies in every color. Then I fell into them"... and that's it. I woke up.

SIMON: Is this the first dream you've recorded?

LUCY: Yes, actually it is.

SIMON: Have you had this dream before?

LUCY: No... not exactly.

SIMON: Something similar?

LUCY: Perhaps... It wasn't exactly like it, but there was another one where I saw him and he was walking away from me.

SIMON: Why do you think that is?

LUCY: I'm not really sure...

SIMON: Lucy, I want you to do me a favor.

LUCY: Yes?

SIMON: Actually, I want you to do yourself a favor.

LUCY: Okay.

SIMON: Lucy, you need to get rid of the alcohol in your house.

LUCY: I've tried.

SIMON: He wouldn't want to see you like this.

LUCY: *(Looking at her arms)* God, if he even knew what I've done...

SIMON: That accident was not your fault, Lucy.

LUCY: That was supposed to be me. I was supposed to be the one behind the wheel, the one lying in the ground as we speak...

SIMON: Why did he go, and not you?

LUCY: I wasn't fit to drive... So he just went out for me as a favor.

SIMON: How did he feel about having to go out?

LUCY: He didn't even want to go... He'd just gotten out of work; there were other things he needed to get done. He said it was the last time he was going to do this. It was a promise that I was going to change.

SIMON: Were you?

LUCY: Yes. *(Pause)* They didn't find him until the early morning. I was at work when they made the call into the ER…

SIMON: Yeah?

LUCY: I saw them bring him in, but the connection didn't hit me.

SIMON: Did you have to work on him?

LUCY: No, they wouldn't let me… They tried everything…

SIMON: How did it make you feel watching them?

LUCY: Like I was the one killed.

SIMON: Did you wish you were with him?

LUCY: *(Softly touching one of the bandages, staring at it)*… Every day

(Lights fade.)

(Lights up on a little café where TODD and RUE sit at a table. They are wearing nicer clothes than what they wore to work. TODD, with possibly his best sweater vest, and RUE with maybe a modest dress. The atmosphere is light.)

TODD: You look… very nice tonight, Rue.

RUE: Thank you…

TODD: You know, the only thing that could possibly make you prettier right now is your smile…

RUE: Todd, shut up.

TODD: What's the matter? Rue, you can tell me anything…

RUE: It's just *Simon*… you know what? Forget it. Let's enjoy ourselves.

TODD: That's what I want to hear. Let's just have fun! Let's just be happy!

RUE: You make me happy.

(They look at one another for a beat, and from the moment, almost on impulse, they both slowly lean in and kiss. It seems at first as if RUE will pull away, but she doesn't. After a quick realization beat, she pulls away immediately.)

RUE: What are you doing?

TODD: I'm sorry! I didn't mean… I'm so sorry, Rue! I…

RUE: I'm sorry. This was a huge mistake. If I had known this was your intent…

TODD: No! No, this wasn't my intent at all, Rue. I swear! I'm sorry, it just happened! I…

RUE: I can't do this… I'll see you at work.

(RUE gets up from the chair and walks away, leaving TODD alone.)

TODD: Rue, please! I'm sorry! *(Pause)* Damn it…

(Lights fade.)

(Lights up in the flower shop the next morning. RUE is alone working on a small arrangement. She doesn't seem to know what she wants to do with it, and is

changing her mind often. After a beat, TODD walks in. He pauses in the doorway when he sees her, but then proceeds to take off his coat and walk into the room. There is an awkward silence about them; almost an internal fight of who should break it first...)

TODD: Good... Morning.

RUE: Morning...

TODD: How was your... uh... morning?

RUE: Well, it *is* fine, thanks.

TODD: Good... good. *(Beat. Simply.)* I'm sorry about last night, Rue. I don't know what came over me. I was never trying to do anything to hurt you, and you know I never would. I didn't mean it and I'm so, *so* sorry. *(Pause)* I understand if you never want to talk to me again...

RUE: I... guess I just don't know what to think.

TODD: Hah, me either...

(The phone rings. Todd answers it.)

Hello, Silva's Flower Shop... yes... *(Immediately brightening)* Oh! Well hello Mr. Scrivello... Yes, yes of course... mmhmm... Next weekend?... We have whatever you want. Something classic, okay... *(RUE moves closes to TODD to try and catch the conversation. He grabs a pen and begins writing.)* Yes... Yes, we do have somebody who can specialize in that... Oh, of course, sir. Our customers will swear by her... Very well sir... Thank you very, *very* much... Alright, you too. Have a wonderful day, Mr. Scrivello. *(TODD hangs up.)*

RUE: Well?

TODD: Nothing.

RUE: Todd, what was that?

TODD: *(Casual)* Oh, nothing. Just Mr. Scrivello.

RUE: What?

TODD: We booked his son's wedding!

RUE: You're kidding! Stephen Scrivello!

TODD: I know!

RUE: This is amazing! *(On impulse, they hug.)*

TODD: And you get to do his bride's bouquet!

(Lights fade.)

(Lights up on RUE sitting at the table. She is smiling and is very anxious and fidgety, waiting for SIMON, who after a beat, walks in. He sets his brief case down, and without much hesitation continues on to find something somewhere in the house. RUE brightens when she sees him, immediately getting up and going to him.)

RUE: Simon! I'm so glad your home! You'll never guess what happened today!

SIMON: Hold on a minute...

(He picks up his briefcase and tries to push past her. She stops him. She's too excited to notice his preoccupation.)

RUE: Oh, please? This will only take a second.

SIMON: Just a minute, *please.*

RUE: We booked the Scrivello wedding!

SIMON: That's nice...

RUE: Their oldest son Martin is getting married and his father...

SIMON: Rue, I don't have time for this...

(He tries to push past her as she tries holding him back to talk.)

RUE: Called us today. They booked *us* to do the flowers for the wedding! I'm making his bride's bouquet!

SIMON: Not now...

RUE: Simon, listen to me for a minute! This wedding is going to be amazing! It's probably the biggest project I've ever gotten. You know what he said? They're going to...

SIMON: Rue!

RUE: Simon, this wedding means a lot to me...

SIMON: You can tell me about it when I get home. Right now I've got to go. I'm running late.

RUE: Simon...

SIMON: I'll be back around 8:30.

(He grabs a manila folder and some papers off the table.)

RUE: Simon, wait...

(He closes the door behind him, leaving her alone. Lights fade.)

(Lights up in the flower shop. It is morning. TODD is sweeping up. After a beat, RUE enters.)

TODD: Morning, Rue.

(RUE goes over to TODD and without warning, kisses him.)

RUE: Morning. *(They break apart and TODD kisses her again, a little longer this time. She breaks away, and goes straight to work without a word.)*

TODD: Umm... the order came in... with the roses Scrivello wanted...

RUE: And?

TODD: He said he wanted you to do up an arrangement.

RUE: But the wedding isn't until next weekend...

TODD: He needs a preview model... everything has to be perfect.

RUE: Perfect... Okay, I can do that.

(Pause. It's burning him. More pause.)

TODD: So uhh... what was that?

RUE: What?

TODD: Uhh well… what are you going to say?

RUE: There's nothing *to* say.

TODD: Wait… so that was… nothing?

RUE: I can just tell Simon. He deals with infidelity all the time. *(Pause)* How ironic is it that his own wife kissed another man?

TODD: *(A little nervous.)* Hah, ironic…

RUE: I think it's funny.

TODD: Funny…

RUE: Well there's no sense in telling him… if you can keep a secret.

(Lights fade.)

(Lights up on RUE and SIMON at the table at their home. It is morning.)

SIMON: I have an extra appointment with a client tonight.

RUE: You have more appointments than any therapist I know.

SIMON: This is serious.

RUE: So what else is new?

SIMON: Don't give me that.

RUE: No, I'm being completely sincere.

SIMON: No, you're not Rue.

RUE: It doesn't matter. *(Pause)* I'm going out tonight.

SIMON: Out?

RUE: Yes, out.

SIMON: Why are you doing that?

RUE: *(Pause)* Because it's my birthday.

(Pause)

SIMON: Oh Rue, I'm so sorry…

RUE: I'm going to be late for work.

SIMON: Rue…

(She leaves as lights fade on SIMON.)

(Lights up on LUCY and SIMON at LUCY'S house. SIMON stands at the table with his briefcase and papers cleaning up.)

LUCY: I'm sorry for all the panic…

SIMON: No, don't be. I don't normally make house calls, but it's no trouble at all, really. Are you feeling better?

LUCY: I really think so… I'm glad we got things taken care of. The last thing I would want is for my brother and his new girlfriend, to see me such a mess.

SIMON: You're doing well. I'm proud of the improvement you're making.

If you need anything - anything at all, again, please don't hesitate to call the office.

(He reaches out to shake her hand.)

LUCY: Thank you very much.

SIMON: And Lucy? Take care of yourself.

LUCY: *(Pause. Smile)* I will... Oh, hey, would you like to stay for dinner?

SIMON: I probably shouldn't...

LUCY: We have more than enough; everything's already made. It's alright if you can't stay; I'm just putting it out there.

SIMON: How about we plan it for another time?

LUCY: I would like that.

SIMON: Wonderful.

(The lights dim on SIMON and LUCY, but the scene remains. Lights up (also) on TODD and RUE. They are outside of LUCY'S house.)

RUE: Are you sure she wants to meet me?

TODD: Are you kidding? You're all I've talked about for weeks.

(In the dim of the house, SIMON dials a number on his cell. RUE takes out her phone and answers.)

RUE: Yes?

(Lights come back up on SIMON in the house. Split stage - or something of the sort. The house location should be more prominent than the outside.)

SIMON: Hey, you...

RUE: Hi, Simon.

SIMON: Surprise. I'm done early.

RUE: Really?

SIMON: Things worked in my favor. There's this new Italian place I've been hearing a lot about. How about it?

RUE: Simon, this is really unexpected. I mean, I'm going out tonight, remember?

SIMON: What are you doing?

RUE: Just... going out.

SIMON: With who?

RUE: A friend. You... wouldn't know her.

TODD: Her?

SIMON: Oh, okay...

RUE: I really want to go with you, but...

SIMON: No, no. You made a commitment. Go out and have a good time. Alright?

RUE: Okay.

SIMON: This weekend though, I'm taking you out for your birthday. I haven't exactly been there for you lately, but starting now, I will. I promise. I'll let you go. Okay? Have fun. I love you. *(RUE hangs up.)*

TODD: What was that about?

LUCY: Would you like a glass of water or anything to drink before you go?

SIMON: Thanks, Lucy. I think I'm all set.

RUE: Nothing... Just Simon.

LUCY: I don't think I could thank you enough for all you've done.

TODD: What about him?

SIMON: It's no problem.

(SIMON goes to his briefcase and looks through the papers. His back is to the door and remains so.)

RUE: I just feel like I shouldn't be here right now...

TODD: You don't have to be nervous... It's going to be okay.

(She smiles and he squeezes her hand in reassurance. TODD knocks on the door.)

LUCY: Coming!

RUE: Well, here goes...

LUCY: *(Opening the door.)* Todd! Hi! Come on in! *(TODD and RUE enter the room. To RUE)* Hi, I'm Lucy, Todd's sister and you must be...

(SIMON turns around and sees RUE who doesn't notice him until he speaks.)

RUE//SIMON: *(Unison)* I'm Rue. // Rue?!?

(Everything goes into panic mode. Lines are quick and overlapped, but clean.)

RUE: ...Simon?!? What are you doing here?

TODD: Oh, God...

SIMON: What am I doing here? What the hell are *you* doing here? And with... him!

RUE: I... uhh...

SIMON: Real cute, Rue. Lucy, I'd like you to meet my *wife*, Ruth.

LUCY: Your wife? What do you mean, I thought...

SIMON: Yes my wife!

RUE: Oh my God...

LUCY: Todd, what have you been doing?!

TODD: What is Simon doing here?

LUCY: He's my therapist!

TODD: I realize that now, but what is he doing at your house?

SIMON: What the hell is this?!?

TODD: Now hold on a minute...

SIMON: If you say another word...

TODD: I...

RUE: Todd, please.

SIMON: Rue, what is this?

RUE: Well, Simon... I uh... I...

SIMON: Well?

RUE: I...

TODD: She's here with me, Simon.

(TODD and SIMON have a moment. SIMON begins to move to attack TODD, but RUE stops SIMON.)

RUE: Don't, please.

SIMON: Why the hell would you do that Rue?

(SIMON advances, but RUE stops him.)

RUE: Stop it, please?!?

SIMON: Just answer my question!!

RUE: Why are you at Lucy's house?

SIMON: Well why are you with Todd? Are you his new girlfriend?

(No response.)

Oh my God... You've got to be *kidding* me! Why in God's name would you do this?!?

RUE: I don't know.

SIMON: Stop lying to me. You cheated on me! With him!

RUE: I'm sorry!

TODD: Don't speak to her like that!

SIMON: This does *not* concern you.

RUE: Todd, just stay out of this...

TODD: You can't let...

RUE: *Please...*

SIMON: I can't believe this!

RUE: Well believe it.

SIMON: How could you do that to me?

RUE: I'm sorry!!

SIMON: Stop telling me you're sorry! What do you have to say for yourself?!

(No response.)

For God sakes Rue, say something!

RUE: I don't know what to say.

(Lights fade.)

(Lights cut to the kitchen of RUE'S home where they continue. This scene shouldn't be a yelling match.)

RUE: I didn't mean for it to happen... it just did!

SIMON: Don't be so damn stupid! Something like this doesn't just... happen!

RUE: He cared about me more than you did.

SIMON: Bullshit! That's the most ridiculous thing I've ever heard.

RUE: He did, Simon!

SIMON: You're acting like this is some sort of game!

RUE: No, I am not!

SIMON: Love is not a game, Ruth. It's not something you play around with! It's a *commitment*! God! I… I can't *believe* you did this to me! Of all the people! I love you! And there was never a time where I didn't! I would never have cheated on you Ruth, and you know it. *(Pause)* Did you…?
(No response.)

Oh, Jesus! Why the hell would you do that!? *Why?!?*

RUE: You left me alone! You left me alone *every single night,* Simon! I couldn't handle it… I can't live *by myself* in this house anymore! You make me feel like I'm worth absolutely nothing to you! You're just lost in your own world while I wait here in what was supposed to be *our* world. Well I've waited, and waited, and I can't wait anymore for you! Simon… I loved you. I loved you more than words could ever express… But I can't be married to somebody who is married to his work. You've made it so much more important than me, Simon. *(Pause)* I can't do this anymore.

SIMON: …loved? *(No response.)* Please don't tell me that…

RUE: I'm sorry…

SIMON: But I love you… I *love you* Rue.

RUE: You don't love me, Simon. You love your work.

SIMON: You *cheated* on me!

RUE: What else was I supposed to do? I needed somebody who was going to be there!

SIMON: Don't give me that shit! Anything I did pales in comparison to what you've done!

RUE: I'm sorry Simon… I don't know what else to do… I don't even know who you are anymore…

SIMON: Rue…

RUE: I want a divorce.

(Lights out.)

(Lights up in the flower shop on TODD and RUE. It is night. RUE has a bag with her.)

TODD: Are you sure you want this?

RUE: I don't. I don't want this at all, Todd. This is never how I wanted to end up…

TODD: You don't have to do this. *(Pause)* I'll leave… and you can stay here with the flowers, and keep your job at Silva's and stay here with… Simon and…

RUE: I've got to go… My bus leaves in ten minutes.

TODD: I'll go with you…

RUE: *(Pause)* This is something I have to do by myself.

TODD: Please don't leave me like this… not now.

RUE: Todd…

TODD: I'm happy, Rue. I'm finally happy and you?

RUE: Todd, please…

TODD: Look, the wedding is tomorrow. This is everything you've worked for. You deserve to be there.

RUE: I just don't think I can…

TODD: I want you to be there. With me. Not as my co-worker or as a friend. Just… listen, give me this. I'm not asking for a promise or, or a commitment. Just one date, one night. And then if you still want to catch that bus, hell, I'll walk you there myself. There will always be another ticket, but… there will never be another chance.

(RUE watches him intently and then her face softens to a small smile.)

RUE: Okay. I will.

TODD: Really?

RUE: Yes.

(He smiles. They embrace. RUE clings to him a bit too long.)

Can you do me a favor?

TODD: Anything.

RUE: Would you go out back and get the bouquet? I'd like to finish it.

TODD: Alright.

(He exits happily. RUE looks around the flower shop, taking everything in. She ultimately makes her decision in this beat and reaches for her bag and quietly makes an exit. After a beat of nothing onstage, TODD re-enters with the bouquet and a smile on his face, which slowly fades when he sees the empty stage. Beat. Lights fade.)

(The End)

Laurel Casillo *as KIM* and Misha Braun *as BRYAN*
in BRYAN AND KIM by Adam Delia.

BRYAN AND KIM

By Adam Delia

Adam Delia is a BA graduate from Marymount Manhattan College, studying acting, studied with James Brill at the Neighborhood Playhouse in a two year Meisner Program, and now takes advanced playwriting with Donna DeMatteo. He's acted and written plays that have been part of the Strawberry Festival (Best Play Award *Bryan and Kim*), Fringe NYC, Fringe Woodstock, and Woodstock Playwrights Union, lead by Wallach Norman. He has also written and directed films like *Goomar,* which was winner of best short film in the Lower East Side Film Festival, and the music video he directed, *Apt. b* was featured on IFC Media Lab.

Bryan and Kim made its world debut on February 6, 2011 in the Strawberry One-Act Festival at the Hudson's Guild Theater in New York, and won Best Play; with the following cast:

BRYAN   Misha Braun
KIM   Laurel Casillo

The play was directed by Adam Delia

CAST OF CHARACTERS

BRYAN, bartender, in his mid to late twenties.
KIM, Bryan's girlfriend, mid twenties.

SCENE I

(*DOWN STAGE are two chairs, both can be the same type of chair or two different types of chairs. UP CENTER STAGE is a bed on a diagonal, making the foot or head of the bed on either side. Lights come up. BRYAN and KIM enter. They walk to their seats and sit down facing audience.*)

KIM: Never really done this before—

BRYAN: So do I start? Or—

KIM: You know, talking to a, you know-

BRYAN: Do you ask a question?—

KIM: A professional. I've never seen a professional before—

BRYAN: I'm actually here for someone else.

KIM: I mean, it's obvious why I'm here—

BRYAN: I mean it's not about me but is.

KIM: I must get points for being here though, right?

BRYAN: I just wanna do the right thing—

KIM: I've never asked for help, never sought out help—

BRYAN: And I didn't know what else to do.

KIM: I've just never been that girl.

BRYAN: Kim was r—

KIM: Bryan's my boyfriend.

BRYAN: Well she's my girl friend—

KIM: We've been dating my almost a year.

BRYAN: And Kim has a past—

KIM: August 24 is our anniversary.

BRYAN: She was...

KIM: And we moved in together.

BRYAN: Christ, I can't even say it.

KIM: We moved in to our new place on June 17.

BRYAN: I mean I don't have to say, if I'm here right?

KIM: Well I moved in to Bryan's place.

BRYAN: Christ— I can't even stand to think of it.

KIM: I'm good with dates, if you couldn't tell.

BRYAN: I don't how she does it—

KIM: And there's another date that is—

BRYAN: But she does.

KIM: Significant.

BRYAN: If it was up to her,

KIM: I should have never told him—

BRYAN: If she had it her way—

KIM: Should've never let him so close.

BRYAN: She would have never told me!

30

KIM: Should've never opened my mouth.

BRYAN: She should be able to tell me anything.

KIM: Let me clear this up saying it wasn't Bryan.

BRYAN: No matter how bad.

KIM: But he's taking it pretty hard.

BRYAN: I just don't know what to do for her. *(Pause)* About a month ago—

KIM: The night was July 14—

BRYAN: We were in bed—

KIM: He had to have that night off from work—

BRYAN: We were watching tv— well, I was watching tv—

KIM: Had to be that exact same night—

BRYAN: Mentally, she was somewhere else.

KIM: And he had to notice—

BRYAN: So I asked what's wrong?

KIM: He asked if I was ok?

BRYAN: She obviously wasn't.

KIM: He had to ask me over and over again.

BRYAN: I couldn't get a straight answer.

KIM: It was too soon.

BRYAN: Then she gets emotional.

KIM: He couldn't take a hint.

BRYAN: She couldn't hide it for shit.

KIM: Just leave it alone.

BRYAN: Now I really wanted her to tell me.

KIM: I was dealing with it on my own.

BRYAN: Very badly might I add.

KIM: Then he started being an asshole.

BRYAN: She was pissing me off.

KIM: It had nothing to do with him.

BRYAN: Then she can tell me what's wrong.

KIM: I didn't wanna scare him off.

BRYAN: *(to KIM)* We live together now.

KIM: Please, it's my problem.

BRYAN: *(to KIM)* You can trust me.

KIM: Not with this— *(BRYAN gets up)* then he got up—

BRYAN: *(to KIM)* I'm going then.

KIM: No, please—

BRYAN: *(to KIM)* Kim, tell me.

KIM: Fine. And then I told him. You see, it was exactly a year ago today, I

was back home, at some party, these two guys, they got me into a room and...
I was raped. *(A MOMENT. She gets up and they are both engaged in the past.)*

BRYAN: Jesus... Are you ok?

KIM: Yeah.

BRYAN: Sorry, that was a dumb question.

KIM: It's fine. It's really not a big deal.

BRYAN: I'm sorry.

KIM: It's ok. You didn't do anything.

BRYAN: I know, but— is there anything I can do?

KIM: There's nothing you can do.

BRYAN: Right, but if there is—

KIM: But nothing. It's ok. I've dealt with it.

BRYAN: You sure?

KIM: Yes, I'm ok now. It's just, we've gotten so close and I didn't wanna
scare you off—

BRYAN: You're not.

KIM: I don't want to lose you.

BRYAN: You won't. I'm glad you told me. *(A moment.)* Do you wanna
talk about it?

KIM: I think I said enough for tonight.

BRYAN: It's ok.

KIM: It's hard for me to talk about it.

BRYAN: I can't even imagine.

KIM: I've never talked about it.

BRYAN: There's nothing you can't tell me—

KIM: I've never told anyone.

BRYAN: You know, that right?

KIM: I just don't want anyone else to know.

BRYAN: Yeah. Of course.

KIM: Just please don't tell anyone.

BRYAN: I won't. But I think you should tell someone.

KIM: I wish I never told you.

BRYAN: No, I told you it's ok.

KIM :It's just embarrassing.

BRYAN: You did nothing wrong.

KIM: Just want it to disappear.

BRYAN: But Kim, it happened.

KIM: I just wanna leave it alone.

BRYAN: Did you report this, right?

KIM: God no!

BRYAN: Why not?!

KIM: I'm not that girl!

BRYAN: What the hell does that mean?!

KIM: It's not something I talk about.

BRYAN: You've kept this in, all this time?

KIM: Bryan, please, it's done.

BRYAN: But if you talk about it—

KIM: I don't want to talk about it!

BRYAN: You deserve some relief.

KIM: It won't give me relief.

BRYAN: I know you're scared—

KIM: No you don't. You don't know shit! *(Pause)* I'm sorry. I didn't mean to yell at you.

BRYAN: No, I'll shut up.

KIM: No, come on. See, this is why I didn't want to tell you, ok? Hey, come here, will ya. *(She holds him, he hugs back.)* I'm sorry.

BRYAN: I'm sorry too, it's just... *(BRYAN & KIM turn to the counselor.)*

BRYAN: I just wish there was something I can do.

KIM: I just wish it can be like the way it was before that night.

BRYAN: That night, our relationship changed.

KIM: Before, when it was just me and him.

BRYAN: But now, it's not just us in our bedroom.

KIM: Now I see them.

BRYAN: You wanna know how it happened?

KIM: My friend Jen calls me telling me there's a party at Matt's house—

BRYAN: It was some keg party with an ex of a friend of her's, who knows.

KIM: It was her ex boyfriend's house and he had some people from the college they go to.

BRYAN: A bunch a frat house guys—

KIM: I met these two guys by the kegs. They were funny.

BRYAN: Later that night when everyone was drunk—

KIM: I had to go the bathroom, and the line on the first floor was long—

BRYAN: So she goes up to the second floor— I guess no one was up there.

KIM: After I use the bathroom, I pass a bedroom—

BRYAN: These two dusch bags are by themselves—

KIM: They've been drinking for awhile—

BRYAN: What the hell was she thinking—

KIM: They showed me some stuff on the internet—

33

BRYAN: Watching porn or some shit!

KIM: So I said I'll leave you two to yourselves—

BRYAN: She didn't call them faggots' or homo's, she didn't even mean it that way.

KIM: And they didn't like that.

BRYAN: And that was it.

KIM: Closed the door on me—

BRYAN: These ignorant fucks—

KIM: They wouldn't let me leave without—

BRYAN: No one even heard her,

KIM: They said they would show me how straight they are.

BRYAN: She was alone with them—

KIM: I don't talk about what happens after that—

BRYAN: She doesn't say much more than that.

KIM: I have no idea how much time went by—

BRYAN: Where the fuck are her friends!?!

KIM: And after I got my clothes and left.

BRYAN: She told no one.

KIM: I didn't say anything.

BRYAN: She didn't report it! Nothing!

KIM: I just left the party.

BRYAN: She's kept this inside.

KIM: I told no one.

BRYAN: And these two spoiled rich trust fund babies get away with this.

KIM: Until I told Bryan.

BRYAN: I just wanna kill these two fucks—

KIM: But, I didn't tell him everything.

BRYAN: She didn't know them.

KIM: I only told him how it happened—

BRYAN: They did this to us.

KIM: I only skimmed the surface.

BRYAN: They did this to her.

KIM: Because no one wants to hear about... it.

BRYAN: Because I'll never really know what it was like.

KIM: I feel like there should be a label on me—

BRYAN: How do you go on with your life after that?

KIM: "Caution, damaged goods."

BRYAN: I mean, when we met, she was fine.

KIM: I wish we can go back to the way it was before that night— *(They both turn to each other in their chairs.)*

34

BRYAN: What can I get ya?

KIM: Can I get a Fuzzy Naval.

BRYAN: Shit. I'm sorry.

KIM: What?

BRYAN: I totally forgot what that is—

KIM: How long have you been bartending?

BRYAN: Long night, as were the last five.

KIM: Oh... sorry. It's vodka, peach shnops and Cranberry.

BRYAN: Ok... —No! That's actually a woo woo.

KIM: A what?

BRYAN: A woo woo, cause a fuzzy naval is the same but with Orange Juice.

KIM: Oh, ok.

BRYAN: So which one do you want?

KIM: What's the cranberry called again?

BRYAN: A woo woo.

KIM: Then I'll have a woo woo.

BRYAN: Ok, here you go.

KIM: Thank you. And sorry about before—

BRYAN: I've never seen you in here—

KIM: I don't really go out.

BRYAN: Where you from?

KIM: Uh— Virginia Beach.

BRYAN: Yeah, how is it there?

KIM: Boring.

BRYAN: A beach?!

KIM: Too many parties— not for me. Where you from?

BRYAN: Right here in Brooklyn.

KIM: You don't sound like you're from Brooklyn—

BRYAN: Thank fuckin' christ! I'm Bryan.

KIM: Kim. How much I owe ya?

BRYAN: Nah, don't worry bout it.

KIM: Are you sure?

BRYAN: Of course I'm sure.

KIM: Ok, thanks.

BRYAN: Hey! Do you wanna hang out sometime, like get some food, or something?

KIM: Uh... I don't really know you.

BRYAN: All the more reason to hang out.

KIM: I— I really can't.

BRYAN: Come on. At least give me your number. I'll beg.

KIM: I don't know if I'm at the right place—
BRYAN: You can make up for giving me a hard time before.
KIM: Which I said I was sorry for—
BRYAN: So give me your number and I can forgive you. *(BOTH turn in their chairs to out.)*
KIM: So I gave him my number.
BRYAN: And I called her—
KIM: Many times.
BRYAN: Not too much.
KIM: He was a persistent little shit!
BRYAN: But eventually—
KIM: I said yes.
BRYAN: And I don't regret any of it.
KIM: But he had no idea what he was in for.
BRYAN: Then things changed. She hasn't been well since—
KIM: Now, I see them all the time.
BRYAN: She has these flashbacks—
KIM: I can't stop it.
BRYAN: She has these... attacks—
KIM: It's been like a flood that kicked in a dam.
BRYAN: And they get physical.
KIM: I try to fight them.
BRYAN: I have to hold her down sometimes.
KIM: I can't control it anymore.
BRYAN: She fights me—
KIM: I lose everything,
BRYAN: Like I'm one of them.
KIM: Like it happened yesterday.
BRYAN: I can't stand being with her when she gets this bad.
KIM: I was thinking, maybe I should let him go.
BRYAN: I have to get away from her.
KIM: Before him, I told no one because I just wasn't that girl.
BRYAN: She can't even admit it sometimes.
KIM: I don't wanna be that girl.
BRYAN: She can't admit it ever.
KIM: I don't wanna tell anyone that I've been—
BRYAN: She got raped!
KIM: But I'm gonna deal with it.
BRYAN: She doesn't know how to deal with this.
KIM: I am dealing with it.
BRYAN: I don't even know how to deal with it.

KIM: He's already done so much for me.

BRYAN: I don't know what to do for her anymore.

KIM: He deserves better.

BRYAN: She didn't deserve this.

KIM: He doesn't need to deal with this.

BRYAN: She should have a normal life.

KIM: He should be with a normal girl.

BRYAN: Normal problems.

KIM: Not someone who is fucked in the head.

BRYAN: She's not fucked up, but it's messing with her.

KIM: I wish I never told him.

BRYAN: *(Looks to her.)* I'm not. I'm glad you told me.

KIM: mmm I should just leave—

BRYAN: What? No, you can't. You can't just leave.

KIM: It would be for the best.

BRYAN: Please don't leave, Kim.

KIM: I'd be dong it for him.

BRYAN: Don't leave me. We can work this out, get better—

KIM: He can do so much better than me—

BRYAN: You are better, better than anything, anyone I've had in a long time. Kim, I love you.

KIM: *(She turns to him.)* No, don't say that, you can't say that—

BRYAN: I wanna say it, I've been wanting to say it—

KIM: No, I don't want you getting hurt—

BRYAN: Then stay.

KIM: Bryan, I—

BRYAN: Please stay.

KIM: Just trust me.

BRYAN: Trust me.

KIM: ...I do.

BRYAN: Then please stay.

KIM: OK. *(She lies on the bed and has an attack of tossing and turning and fighting them off.)*

BRYAN: I'm lucky, because I can leave, go for a walk and won't have to think about this. But she doesn't have a choice in the matter. I can see it in her. At night she can't sleep, she's exhausted in the morning. Our sex life was good until now. She still wants sex and I just hope it takes her mind off it for ten, twenty minutes; but now these two bastards have entered our lives, even our most intimate moments— it happens now all the time— *(By this time, BRYAN has gotten up and has made his way to the bed to lay.)*

BRYAN: OWWWW.

KIM: Sorry. Are you ok?—
BRYAN: I'm fine. It's fine—
KIM: I'm sorry.
BRYAN: It's not a big deal.
KIM: You're back! Oh Bryan, I'm sorry!
BRYAN: Really, you don't need to worry about it.
KIM: Are you mad at me?
BRYAN: It's not your fault—
KIM: So you are angry?
BRYAN: No—
KIM: You just said that it's not my fault—
BRYAN: I know what I said.
KIM: You can tell me anything.
BRYAN: I'm sure I can!
KIM: What?
BRYAN: Nothing.
KIM: No, what did I do?
BRYAN: Don't worry about it.
KIM: Maybe I should go.
BRYAN: Don't start with that again!
KIM: I'm not, but I know it can get difficult—
BRYAN: It's just...
KIM: Yeah?
BRYAN: You need to start seeing someone professional—
KIM: I'm not ready for that—
BRYAN: I think we should start getting you some help—
KIM: No! I don't want that.
BRYAN: You need to start talking to a therapist.
KIM: Not yet.
BRYAN: Ok. When?
KIM: Excuse me?
BRYAN: When will you be ready?
KIM: Don't ask me that.
BRYAN: Well, you gotta make a decision.
KIM: Don't give me some dead line!
BRYAN: Kim, it wouldn't be bad idea—
KIM: No.
BRYAN: I'll look stuff up for you. I'll find someone—
KIM: No Bryan!
BRYAN: I think you're ready to take the next step.
KIM: I'm not.

BRYAN: Well you have to do something.

KIM: I'll make that decision for myself.

BRYAN: Ok, fine. I'm sorry. It's just...

KIM: What?

BRYAN: I don't know how to say this—

KIM: Then just say it.

BRYAN: Where are you during sex?

KIM: What?

BRYAN: Where is your mind?

KIM: With you—

BRYAN: No, it's not. You've been really aggressive lately.

KIM: I'm sorry I scratched your back—

BRYAN: No. It's more than that... do you have any idea what I'm talking about?

KIM: Just tell me.

BRYAN: When you're having an attack, a flashback; you do the same thing during...

KIM: I don't get what you're saying—

BRYAN: During sex... you look like... like you're getting...

KIM: Bryan!?

BRYAN: It feels like I'm raping you! *(Pause.)*

KIM: I don't know what to say to that.

BRYAN: You've never noticed this?

KIM: It felt like you were raping me?

BRYAN: I didn't know how to tell you.

KIM: We never stopped. You always finished.

BRYAN: Wait, what?

KIM: I don't remember you ever stopping yourself.

BRYAN: Well, I mean—

KIM: Did it help?

BRYAN: What?!

KIM: Did you use it?

BRYAN: No!

KIM: Did you like it?

BRYAN: What the hell is this?!

KIM: Where was your mind, Bryan?

BRYAN: I wasn't raping you, Kim!

KIM: I'm gonna go now.

BRYAN: I don't want that.

KIM: I don't care what you want.

BRYAN: You don't want that—

KIM: You have no idea what I want! So stop talking to me like some little kid!

BRYAN: I'm only trying to help.

KIM: I don't want your help.

BRYAN: Kim—

KIM: Bye Bryan. *(BRYAN begins to exit, when they both go to their counselor seats.)*

BRYAN: I just wanted to help. I don't think I can help. *(BRYAN goes and sits on the bed.)*

KIM: See, I've never needed anything from anyone— I never wanted pity, I want to be treated like everyone else. I'm not some victim. I'm not gonna cry about it for the rest of my life. I gotta move on. That's what I hate about Bryan, he just dwells on things, like this; what's it gonna do, you know? I know he's trying to help, and he wants the best for me, but I've never been that girl— God! *(She looks at him.)* What has this been doing to him? *(She sees BRYAN on the bed. She goes to him.)*

KIM: Are you ok?

BRYAN: Yeah.

KIM: I'm sorry.

BRYAN: It's fine.

KIM: No it's not. I was wrong.

BRYAN: I don't know. It's like— I see you, and there's nothing I can do—

KIM: Look at me, you do help me. You have helped me. You're the best thing that's happened to me in a really long time—

BRYAN: But Kim, it's not enough!

KIM: What do you mean?

BRYAN: I mean I can't do this every night.

KIM: I know—

BRYAN: It's too much.

KIM: I know Bryan—

BRYAN: I know you know; you say you know; but it's doesn't help anymore!

KIM: What do you want me to do?

BRYAN: I'll go with you Kim.

KIM: Bryan, I can't do that—

BRYAN: I'll go with you, or I'll go with out you—

KIM: I've never been that girl—

BRYAN: Kim, please— we're not gonna last very long.

KIM: ...Ok.

BRYAN: Yeah?

KIM: Ok, I'll get help. I will.
BRYAN: We both will. *(They hug and then head to their seats.)*
KIM: Never really done this before—
BRYAN: So do I start? Or—
KIM: You know, talking to a, you know—
BRYAN: Do you ask a question?—
KIM: A professional. I've never seen a professional before—
BRYAN: I'm actually here for someone else.
KIM: I mean, it's obvious why I'm here—
BRYAN: I mean it's not about me...but is.
KIM: I must get points for being here though, right?
BRYAN: I just wanna do the right thing—
KIM: I've never asked for help, never sought out help—
BRYAN: And I didn't know what else to do.
KIM: I've just never been that girl.

(Lights Fade to Black.)
(The End)

Amanda B. Goodman *as REBECCA*, William Metcalfe *as NARRATOR*
Hazen Cuyler *as NOAH*, Alex West *as TIM*,
and Carson Dougherty *as HALLIE*
in LOVE FOR BEGINNERS by Cesar Abella.

LOVE FOR BEGINNERS

By Cesar Abella

Cesar Abella is the winner of the Old Vic New Voices Out of Character Monologue Competition. A native of San Francisco, he received his BA in Theater from UCLA and his MA in Writing for Stage and Broadcast Media from The Central School of Speech and Drama, London. He has written extensively for Old Vic New Voices at The Old Vic in London and is a founding member of Straight Out of Lone Company. Love for Beginners was his audition piece for The Old Vic's 24 Hour Plays 2009.

Love for Beginners had its world premiere on July 30, 2011, at The Hudson Guild Theatre, New York City, as part of The Strawberry One-Act Festival as presented by The Riant Theatre with the following cast, in order of appearance:

NOAH	Hazen Cuyler
REBECCA	Amanda B. Goodman
TIM	Alex West
HALLIE	Carson Dougherty
NARRATOR	William Metcalfe

The play was directed by Jonathan Song Chang and stage managed by Jenny Waletzky.

CAST OF CHARACTERS

NOAH, a twenty-year-old geeky college student.
HALLIE, a pretty college student in her early twenties.

REBECCA, an aggressive college student in her early twenties.
TIM, a good-looking jock college student in his early twenties.
NARRATOR, any gender, any age.

TIME: The late 1990s.
SCENE: An urban collegiate wasteland.

(NOAH, geeky boy of 20, stands, facing out. Behind him, three people: HALLIE, REBECCA, and TIM, all standing apart.)

REBECCA: You can't get it up, and you cry and I cry and I get / frustrated.

TIM: I've never done something like that before. But I've / wanted to.

HALLIE: You're gonna make some girl very happy one day.

(A NARRATOR enters, watching Noah. Then, the NARRATOR begins. As the NARRATOR speaks, the other four disappear.)

NARRATOR: The first time Noah kissed a girl, he was five years old. The sensation was one that he carried with him for the rest of his life. The August sun against his forearms, the sand of the playground underneath his knees, Ellen Halloran's soft lips against his. But he turned and ran, and to this day, he wondered if he would do the same thing if opportunity struck again.

(A staircase outside an apartment. There is a party going on inside. HALLIE sits crying on the steps. A moment later, NOAH steps out. He sees her, unsure what to do, then sits down next to her.)

NOAH: Hallie? *(She keeps crying.)* Are you okay?

HALLIE: *(Looking up.)* Hello? Oh, Noah. Um… yeah, I'm fine. Don't mind me. I just like to cry for fun sometimes. Especially at parties.

NOAH: Oh. Do you find crying fun? I find roller coasters fun, personally, but if there's a benefit in crying, please let me know and I'll try it. Then again, I don't really cry on my own. I need to, like, punch myself a few times. Or talk to my dad. He makes me cry.

(She starts wailing again and puts her head in her arms. The NARRATOR enters.)

NARRATOR: It was at this particular moment that Noah realized that Hallie wasn't being serious about crying for fun. Noah never had much interaction with girls, even at his advanced age of twenty. However, something inside him that he couldn't explain prompted him to act.

(NOAH tentatively puts a hand on Hallie's back and rubs it.)

NOAH: Whatever it is, Hallie, it's okay.

(She looks up at him. She grabs his hand without thinking. He tries not to react to this.)

HALLIE: Thanks a lot, Noah. Really.

NOAH: Was a guy mean to you? Who is it? I'll go... do something. I'll punch him out. Or, I mean, he'll probably punch *me* out first, but I'll throw a lot of big words at him that he won't understand.

(HALLIE giggles.)

HALLIE: Noah. Why aren't we friends?

NOAH: *(Imitating a robot.)* I'm a robot. The word "friend" does not compute.

HALLIE: *(Laughing louder.)* You're funny.

NOAH: Funny-looking, right?

HALLIE: You know, you're gonna make some boy very happy one day.

NOAH: Some... boy?

HALLIE: Yeah. You're gay, right, Noah?

NOAH: No. I'm not.

HALLIE: Oh! I mean, did I offend you or... I'm so sorry!

NOAH: Don't worry about it. Everybody thinks I'm gay. The aforementioned dad who makes me cry? He does. I'm used to it. It doesn't bother me.

HALLIE: Well. You're gonna make some girl very happy one day.

NOAH: Maybe. Hopefully.

HALLIE: Yeah.

(They look at each other, then look away.)

HALLIE: *(Standing)* I'm going back inside. I'll see you in there?

NOAH: Yeah. And, um... you owe me a dance.

HALLIE: Yeah. I do.

(She exits. NOAH does a dorky dance of sorts, smiling to himself.)

NARRATOR: And that was how it started between Noah and Hallie. A phone call here, an AOL conversation there, ultimate frisbee games, Pop-Up Video marathons, and eventually three dates in one week. Classmates would watch them walking hand in hand and think confusedly to themselves about how such a pair was formed. Two months into the romance, Noah grew up a little bit.

(NOAH and HALLIE entwined on the sofa. Noah's head is on Hallie's shoulder.)

NOAH: Hey. So I've been thinking.

HALLIE: What did I tell you about thinking?

NOAH: I... I think... I think I'm in love with you.

HALLIE: What?

NOAH: Yeah. *(Pause)* Was that stupid of me to say? Shit. Um... let's forget it. I'm, um, yeah. Are you hungry?

(He stands up, but she pulls him back down.)

NOAH: I can make us pasta, maybe. Or eggs. Or...

HALLIE: Stop talking. You're such a girl.

(She kisses him.)

NARRATOR: Then, the day came when Noah became a man.

HALLIE: We need to talk.

NOAH: Uh-oh. Bad conversations always start off with "we need to talk."

HALLIE: I, um… I don't know how to say this. *(Pause)* We, um… I'm not… feeling this anymore.

NOAH: What do you mean?

HALLIE: This, uh… this has to be… shit! I think I wanna, um, break up with you.

NOAH: Oh.

HALLIE: Yeah.

NOAH: Really?

HALLIE: Yeah.

NOAH: But I love you. I want us to get married.

HALLIE: I… don't.

NOAH: What about… What about…?

HALLIE: You're gonna make some girl very happy one day.

(She walks away.)

NARRATOR: Noah tried to convince himself that he was over Hallie, that she had been completely wrong for him and would have subsequently ruined his life. *She likes Yahoo!, but obviously Netscape is better,* he would think. *Paula Cole better than Fiona Apple? Please!* But none of these statements made him stop crying, not even as he chatted away with random girls on AOL dating chat rooms. However, to mend his broken heart, Noah trudged on until he found himself having a coffee with a girl named Rebecca.

(NOAH and REBECCA at a coffee shop. He walks in and sees her. He walks over to her.)

NOAH: Hey. Rebecca?

REBECCA: SunnyGirl316. Are you WeezerBot1701?

NOAH: Noah. Yeah. Yeah.

(He hugs her awkwardly and super-awkwardly kisses her. She is taken aback, but doesn't dislike it.)

NOAH: Oh. Shit. Um. I wasn't… I'm so sorry. I don't… I don't know what…

REBECCA: It's okay. Um… Let's… Let's take it as a good omen.

NOAH: Yeah. Okay.

(They sit down.)

NOAH: So, this is a nice place, right? I really like the whole décor scheme. Like this, you know, Arts and Crafts thing they have going on here.

(HALLIE appears behind Noah.)
    HALLIE: Oh no.
    REBECCA: *(Simultaneous.)* Oh no.
    HALLIE: Don't start with the interior design, Noah. Now she thinks you're —
    REBECCA: I'm sorry, but… are you gay?
    NOAH: What?
    REBECCA: You know, gay. Like a homosexual. Like, you're sitting here with me, but you're secretly fantasizing that I was a dude?
    NOAH: What? No. No!
    REBECCA: Are you sure?
    NOAH: Why would you say that?
    HALLIE: What straight guy comments / on interior design?
    REBECCA: What straight guy comments on interior design?
    NOAH: Oh. It's just, you know, I, uh, have a… a collection of —
    HALLIE: Don't say it.
    NOAH: – Crate & Barrel… catalogs…?
    REBECCA: Crate & Barrel catalogs.
    NOAH: It's a pretty substantial collection.
    REBECCA: Really.
    NOAH: If you want, we can, like, go back to my place and look at them…?
    REBECCA: Okay. Alright. I'm out of here.
    NOAH: Wait. No.
    REBECCA: Look, it's clear that you're in some serious denial and —
    NOAH: I'm not! I mean —
    REBECCA: You don't understand. Gay boys break my heart. All the time.
    NOAH: I'm sorry —
    REBECCA: I've done this before. And I know how it will turn out. Your parents don't talk to you because of who you are and you're trying really hard to be able to talk to them. So you're looking for a girlfriend. So we start dating and everything's fun because we can watch *Shakespeare in Love* and eat Haagen-Dasz and cuddle and share really sweet kisses. But then I want to have sex, and you can't get it up, and you cry and I cry and I get frustrated and cuss you out and then I take you to the Christmas party at work and I catch you blowing one of my co-workers in an empty office while I'm looking for the bottle of vodka I snuck in. And it'll suck and I don't want to be part of that.
    NOAH: But —
    REBECCA: I can't afford to do this to myself.
    NOAH: I won't be like that.

REBECCA: I gotta go. Good luck with your search.
(She stands and leaves. HALLIE leans in to NOAH.)
HALLIE: I didn't like her hair. It looks like it's just you and me here.
NARRATOR: Thus ended Rebecca. But the online dates didn't stop, nor did Noah's quest to find someone to vanquish the visions of Hallie from his mind. She appeared on every single date, watched over every single encounter, judged, smiled, and made Noah miss her incredibly. Then, one day, Noah decided to have a drink with his friend, Tim, whom he hadn't seen for a long time.
(NOAH and TIM sitting, drinking and drunk.)
NOAH: So, it's just like... stupid girls! I hate them!
TIM: They are so mean.
NOAH: I know!
TIM: I know!
NOAH: It is so nice to, just, like, have someone to just... talk to.
TIM: Yeah. It's been, how long, dude?
NOAH: Like, three years.
TIM: Jesus.
NOAH: I know!
TIM: Yeah. I don't... I don't have a lot of friends, really. It gets a bit lonely away at school.
NOAH: I didn't know that. But good-looking guy like you. Should have girls on each arm.
TIM: No, no. Not me. I... I don't do that.
NOAH: Ha! Me neither. But then again, I look like Quasimodo on a good day.
TIM: That's not true, Noah. You're... you're good-looking, too.
NOAH: Shut the fuck up.
TIM: No, really. Cute, actually.
(They look at each other. TIM kisses NOAH.)
NARRATOR: After having heard all his life that he was gay, Noah tried to experience this moment and take everything in, to see if in fact something happened that had never happened with girls before, something that could silence the past. The past, however, couldn't have picked a worse time to appear.
(HALLIE and REBECCA appear.)
REBECCA: I knew it! I knew it the whole time!
HALLIE: Oh God. I hope I didn't do this to him.
REBCCA: Giving yourself a little too much credit, aren't we, dear?
HALLIE: Don't be jealous because I'm more special to him than you'll ever be. *(Pause)* Why *are* you here anyway? You went on one date with him!

(NOAH and TIM break the kiss. NOAH stands up.)

TIM: What's wrong?

NOAH: I, uh... What was that?

TIM: It... it felt like the thing to do.

NOAH: Did it?

TIM: Yes.

HALLIE: Noah, why is she here? I thought maybe that girl who went to Olive Garden with you would be here. I don't like this one.

REBECCA: Noah, I've been waiting for the day. And it's finally here. I was right the whole time. *(Looks to HALLIE.)* You owe me ten bucks, I believe.

NOAH: I don't... I don't know.

TIM: I... I've never done something like that before.

NOAH: Me, neither.

TIM: But I've wanted to.

NOAH: Really?

TIM: Yes. With you.

NOAH: Why?

TIM: I've missed you.

NOAH: I'm... I'm a nobody.

TIM: Not to me.

(TIM walks over to NOAH. He pus his arms around him, but NOAH slowly takes them off.)

NOAH: I... I can't, Tim. I'm sorry.

TIM: Why not?

NOAH: I'm... I'm not gay.

HALLIE: Ha! *(Looks to REBECCA.)* Give me back my money, honey!

TIM: This sucks.

NOAH: It does.

NARRATOR: The past can hold on to you in ways that you can't even imagine. Noah's mind became a shrine to the mistakes and the follies and the embarrassment.

(HALLIE, REBECCA, and TIM stand behind NOAH.)

TIM: Hmm. This is an interesting place, isn't it?

REBECCA: It's boring. I have no idea why I'm here.

HALLIE: Me, neither. And I'm really sick of you. *(To TIM)* You, however... It's such a shame you're gay.

REBECCA: I still think Noah is. My gaydar is pinging like crazy.

HALLIE: Noah loved me. Still does. Always will.

TIM: Well, obviously I'm important enough to be here. I really wish he loved me.

REBECCA: I wasn't going to let him break my heart.

HALLIE: Noah...

TIM: Noah...

REBECCA: Noah...

(NOAH stands up and looks at them.)

NOAH: Shut up! All of you! Shut up and get out of my life, please?!

(They're all a bit shocked.)

TIM: Being a bit dramatic, aren't we?

HALLIE: See, Noah, these campy Joan Crawford meltdowns aren't helping you in the masculinity department.

NOAH: I... I can't keep hearing you guys. You just talk and talk and *talk* my fucking balls off, about this and that and "Noah, stop doing that" or "Noah, why is she here?" or "Noah, your hips have no rhythm, no wonder you never get laid" and I'm up to *here* with it. *(Pause)* I never thought I'd say this, but... I want you gone. All of you.

REBECCA: You don't want me around?

NOAH: No. Go away.

REBECCA: Finally. I always wondered why I was here. We didn't even make it to dinner. It was the briefest date I've ever been on, and that's including the random hook-up in a bathroom I had once.

NOAH: Wait, really?

REBECCA: No. The real me isn't as evil as you imagine me to be. But I wasn't going to end up single one day and have you watching over each of my dates. I didn't want you to be my Hallie.

NOAH: I don't know what you mean.

REBECCA: See? Our conversations would have sucked.

(She disappears.)

TIM: These girls are really mean.

NOAH: I'm a sucker for masochism.

TIM: I wouldn't have been mean to you. You know that.

NOAH: I know.

TIM: It would have been fun. We coulda gone to baseball games and then made out afterwards.

NOAH: It coulda been fun.

TIM: You think that maybe in the future...?

NOAH: I don't know.

TIM: Well. I'll see you around, Noah.

(He disappears.)

NOAH: Bye, Scarecrow. I'll miss you most of all.

HALLIE: What straight guy casually drops *Wizard of Oz* quotes into everyday conversation?

NOAH: I do.

HALLIE: I know. It's cute.

NOAH: I will miss you. You were my first... everything.

HALLIE: You'll live. Just try it.

(She disappears.)

NOAH: *(Becoming more and more unsure)* They're gone. They're gone. They're... gone. They're. Gone. Gone.

(He turns around and realizes that he is alone. He doesn't seem so sure about this.)

NARRATOR: We meet hundreds of people in our lives. And we fall in love with a few of them. If we're lucky, they love us back. But every scar that they inflict upon us, every scar we inflict upon them, is etched forever on our brain. And a simple request to forget them, to have them leave us will be met with a silence so deafening that a simple whisper can sound like someone making a crude rip through expensive fabric. The bruises will always follow us, taunting and teasing, begging us to accept them for what they are – part of the journey.

(NOAH stands and looks out as before. For a brief second, HALLIE, REBECCA, and TIM reappear.)

> *(Lights out.)*
> *(The end.)*

Will Budnikov *as MIKOS,* Jane E. Hagerty *as DEBRA STEINHART,*
Amanda Gordon *as MARGE,*
Ian Matthew Cutler *as MANNY STEINHART*
and Brenda Hoffman *as SELMA STEINHART*
in IT'S GREEK TO ME by Shelly A. Bromberg

IT'S GREEK TO ME

By Shelley A. Bromberg

Shelley A. Bromberg is a playwright, actress, singer/songwriter, and educator. She recently completed a romantic comedy screenplay *My Best Man*. She holds a M.A. in Communication Arts from Montclair State University and a B.A. in Speech and Theatre Education from the University of Maryland at College Park. She is a certified teacher of theatre, speech, and English and has taught at the college, high school, and middle school levels.

It's Greek to Me made its New York City debut on July 30, 2011 at the Hudson Guild Theatre. It was a semi-finalist and received a best actor nomination in The Riant Theatre's Summer 2011 Strawberry One-Act Festival with the following cast, in order of appearance:

SELMA STEINHART	Brenda Hoffman
MIKOS	Will Budnikov
MARGE	Amanda Gordon
MANNY STEINHART	Ian Matthew Cutler
DEBRA STEINHART	Jane E. Hagerty

The play was directed by Michael Z. Murphy.

CAST OF CHARACTERS

SELMA STEINHART, 50's. She is loving, indecisive and lost.
MIKOS, 20's-30, well-built, bronze, and handsome with a well-defined Mediterranean look. Has versatility and flair with members of the opposite sex, speaks with accent.

MANNY STEINHART, Selma's son, physically big, overweight, loud, immature and inappropriate on the outside, teddy bear on the inside.

DEBRA STEINHART, wife of Manny. Kind and well-meaning wife and daughter-in-law, has never achieved any schooling beyond high school nor has she traveled abroad. Unlike Manny, she has a maturity and appropriateness about her.

MARGE, down-to-earth, good friend, New York type, honest to a point: what you see is what you get. Unique by voice or physical appearance, age can vary 50's – 80's.

SCENE I

(Jewish tombstone of Solomon Steinhart in tranquil cemetery. SELMA places stone on tombstone.)

SELMA: My beloved Solomon. *(She kisses fingers then touches stone.)* Do you know what today is? That's right. Today was your unveiling. I hope you like the stone. Manny and I picked it out. You know our precious son went to shul every single day to say kaddish for you. Do you like my dress? This shade is called cloudy sky gray. I don't have to wear black anymore. You know, we lived our lives in the well-defined circle for twenty-five glorious years. Thank you for that. I'm sorry that in the end, I just couldn't do more. Sitting by your side at the hospital and being with your during your treatments, just wasn't enough. And as you drifted further away from me, from us, I couldn't hold on. And I moved into an undefined gray area outside of the circle and here I stay. *(She pulls out envelope from purse.)* Manny and Debra thought it was a good idea for me to get away for a while. I wonder where they have in mind. *(She opens envelope containing ticket and brochure.)* It's a single ticket to Greece. You know it was always our dream to go there together. I don't want to disappoint Manny and Debra. They've been so kind to me. Is it okay with you if I go? Give me a sign my love, and I will do whatever you wish. *(She reads brochure.)* "Explore Athens and the Greek Isles. It's all within your reach when you travel with Solomon tours." *(She laughs.)* Solomon Tours. You always did have a knack for timing. Thank you, my love. So, I guess I won't be here for a while. Until I return, rest peacefully, my love. *(She picks up pebble, puts in pocket, and departs.)*

SCENE II

(Food stand in Greek market place. SELMA enters, dressed in a primary solid color, and weighted down in bags.)

MIKOS: So, Madam, what you like?

SELMA: I don't know. There are so many delightful choices. Hmm. What is in that one? Is that spinach?

MIKOS: This is spanakopita, favorite dish of famous American Greeks: George Stephanopolis, Olympia Dukakis, and Alex Rodriguez. Let me assist. *(He removes bag from Selma's shoulder.)*

SELMA: Thanks. Wow! Span-i-ko-pi-ta! I love this language. And what is that?

MIKOS: This is tzatziki (dza-dzee'kee).

SELMA: Tza-tzi-ki. (dza-dzee'kee)

MIKOS: Yogurt, cucumber, and garlic dip- favorite voice warm up of American Greek singers, Frank Zappa, Constantine Maroulis, Deepak Chopra. *(He removes another bag from Selma's shoulder.)*

SELMA: Thank you. And this?

MIKOS: A fine Greek pastry, baklava.

SELMA: Bak-la-va.

(MIKOS pops a piece into her mouth to sample.)

MIKOS: There is legend that even from small bite, a fine Mykonos native can fall instantly in love with you. Just like Aristotle Onassis and Jackie O.

SELMA: Really!

MIKOS: So, what you like, Lady? As you Americans love to say, "All of the day, my handsome camel does not spend in my fine, silk pajamas." Let me assist. *(He removes the rest of the bags.)*

SELMA: Thanks. I just can't decide.

MIKOS: I will assist. Here in Mykonos, we delight the palate with a little bit of everything. Olives, some fine, ripened retsina; red wine, tyropita, feta cheese, and my favorite, moussaka. Here you are. *(He hands her package.)* Enjoy your stay.

SELMA: Thank you!

SCENE III

(Tired, with sore feet, and encumbered with bags, Selma spots a bathhouse and enters cautiously. There is a massage table draped with a sheet. Mikos enters.)

SELMA: You?

MIKOS: I am man of many trades. For what are you here? Let me assist. *(He removes bag.)*

SELMA: Thanks. What are the choices?

MIKOS: Greek folk dance, belly dance, meditation, massage and foot reflexology, electrolysis… I can assist. *(He removes bag.)*

SELMA: Wait, wait, what was that?

MIKOS: You want hair removed?

SELMA: No, before that one.

MIKOS: Massage and foot reflexology

SELMA: Yes, that's it.

MIKOS: Take off your clothes.

SELMA: Excuse me?

MIKOS: You want full Mediterranean experience?

SELMA: No, just the foot reflexology, thank you.

MIKOS: But Madam, I cannot do my job.

SELMA: I am sure you can do your job just fine.

MIKOS: Yes, with your clothes off. Please lay face up and cover with towel.

(Selma puts down pebble, undresses, places towel around her, and lies down. He reveals each body part as needed.)

SELMA: Just work on my feet.

(He begins massaging feet.)

MIKOS: What goes on here anyway?

MIKOS: What do you think?

SELMA: I've heard rumors about these kinds of places.

MIKOS: Rumor? What is rumor?

SELMA: Stories, you know, about the men and the women. Especially American women. And I've heard stories about the men and the men, and the women and the women.

MIKOS: Tell me what you hear. *(He starts massaging a leg.)*

SELMA: Stick to the feet. My feet! They are below my ankles.

(He rubs feet then starts lathering her arms with oils.)

SELMA: What is that?

MIKOS: Gentle pressure with grapeseed oil.

SELMA: Ahhh. That feels nice. Why do you think European men cheat on their wives so much? Stick to the feet.

MIKOS: I did not know that they do. *(He massages her feet.)*

SELMA: What is your name?

MIKOS: You can call me Mikos.

SELMA: What does that mean I can call you that? Is that your real name?

MIKOS: American women, so suspicious.

SELMA: Mikos, I feel a spasm in thigh.

MIKOS: Yes, we must work the thigh. *(He massages thigh.)* A lot of pressure here.

SELMA: Ahh. That feels divine.

MIKOS: So, what is your name?

SELMA: You can call me Desdemona.

MIKOS: Desdemona, it is my pleasure to make your acquaintance.

SELMA: You too. I bet you've been with loads of women. They come away to this beautiful island, looking for a good time —

MIKOS: Is that why you are here?

SELMA: Me? No, I'm what you call old school: I only love and care for one at a time.

MIKOS: In Mykonos, You are like pearl in oyster. See if this takes out tension. *(He starts massaging her back.)*

SELMA: Yes, that is good. Very good.

MIKOS: A lot of tension and stress here.

SELMA: Ahh, yes. Then return to the feet.

(MIKOS returns to massaging feet.)

MIKOS: So you are beautiful woman exploring Greece alone. *(He begins massaging her shoulder and neck.)*

SELMA: Well, I'm on a tour, of course.

MIKOS: Of course. Here in Mykonos, we delight the body with a little bit of everything.

SELMA: I think I'm going to enjoy my stay in Mykonos.

MIKOS: What will be your pleasure?

SELMA: Is there more?

MIKOS: As we say, for beautiful woman, the cup of white wine runneth over.

SELMA: Then I will have a full cup.

MIKOS: Then it is settled.

SELMA: What's settled? What are you talking about?

MIKOS: You and I will partake in Greek delight.

SELMA: We will? What is that, Greek delight? It sounds so exotic.

Lights out.

SELMA: Oh, Mikos? Mikos! Mikos!

SCENE IV

MANNY: Blessed art thou, Oh Lord our God, King of the Universe, who brings forth grapes from the vine.

ALL: Amen.

(The lights come up. A Passover Seder. Dining room table has a lacey tablecloth with plastic cover. The table is set with traditional Seder plate, matzo, and wine. Everyone sits around table. MANNY has arm around DEBRA. Selma is dressed in wild colors. There is an empty seat for the Prophet Elijah.)

MARGE: Selma, thank you for inviting me for the holiday.

(SELMA stares off distantly.)

MANNY: Ma, what's up with you?

SELMA: Oh, nothing! Yes, my dear, Mikos, Marjorie, I'm so happy you could join us.

MANNY: Ma, we're done with the prayers. You can bring up the food now, and don't forget to open the door for the Prophet Elijah.

SELMA: Oh, okay. The food should be hot by now. I'll go check. *(She heads downstairs.)*

DEBRA: Let me give you a hand, Ma.

SELMA: it's okay. I got it.

MANNY: So, Marge. May I ask you a personal question?

MARGE: Sure.

MANNY: How much did you pay for that blouse?

DEBRA: Manny, you don't need to know that.

MARGE: It's okay. Uh, I don't know. Maybe thirty bucks.

MANNY: Aha. I knew it. You know you could have gotten something like it cheaper at Deb's shop.

DEBRA: Manny, if Marge wants to come to the store she can. You don't have to –

MANNY: I'm tryin' to promote your business, Debbie. What's wrong with you?

MARGE: Actually, that's a great idea. Maybe I could stop in later in the week.

MANNY: SEE?

(SELMA returns from downstairs.)

SELMA: Here we are! Time for soup! Is there a blessing for this? Let me go check on the entrees.

DEBRA: Ma, sit down and relax already. You're wearing yourself out.

SELMA: My dear Sol, may he rest in peace, wanted a second kitchen in the basement that would be kosher for Passover, and it's been this way for years. It's okay. I got it.

(She heads down.)

MANNY: Deb, you gotta try my coleslaw. Marge, do you like coleslaw? Do one thing for me. Just try it.

(DEBRA tastes it and starts choking.)

DEBRA: Whoa... what's in that?

MANNY: Whole pepper corns! What do ya say, Marge?

MARGE: I'm not a coleslaw kind of gal.

MANNY: What kind of gal are ya? *(Flirting)* Maybe you could tell me later.

DEBRA: You don't put whole peppercorns into coleslaw!

MANNY: Why not? It's my secret ingredient.

(SELMA returns a little more drained.)

SELMA: The food is hot! I ordered brisket, roasted turkey, potato kugel, broccoli kugel, beat salad—

MANNY: Ma, why did you order the broccoli kugel again? Nobody ate it last year.

SELMA: I don't know. Moshani (Mo shon' ee) gives me the wrong order every year.

MANNY: Then why do you keep ordering from him?

SELMA: My dear Marjorie, you do like broccoli don't you?

MARGE: Sure, sure. *(She grimaces at DEBRA.)*

MANNY: The potato kugel is horrible.

SELMA: Really? Oh, I almost forgot one more thing. *(She jumps up.)*

MANNY: Ma, would ya sit down already? The food's gonna get cold.

SELMA: This is a special dish I made just for this occasion. Carry on. *(She heads down.)*

MANNY: Hey Marge, do you know how to keep a sex maniac in suspense?

MARGE: I give up. How?

MANNY: Never mind. I'll tell ya next week. *(MANNY explodes into buckets of laughter.)* I gotcha. I gotcha, Marge.

MARGE: You did, Manny. Very good. *(Grimaces.)*

DEBRA: What was that?

MANNY: What?

DEBRA: Why are you telling a sex joke and on Passover no less?

MARGE: *(Under her breath.)* Like this night is different from any other.

MANNY: What's wrong with that?

DEBRA: Just forget it.

MANNY: No tell me. What is wrong with that joke? Marge liked it. Didn't ya, Marge?

MARGE: *(Deadpan)* It was very funny.

DEBRA: I shouldn't have to explain it to you.

MANNY: Explain what?

DEBRA: Marge is a friend of your Mother's.

MANNY: Yeah and?

DEBRA: And she's of a mature age.

MANNY: So, I tell dirty jokes to old ladies. Ma volunteers me at nursing homes. The ladies are old, their boobs are sagging and they need some uplifting. Get it, Marge. Uplifting?

MARGE: I get it.

MANNY: I ballroom dance with them. I remember one old hag. She smelled like a combination of carnations and formaldehyde. I asked her "How do you keep a sex maniac in suspense?" Had I been wearing a toupe when I dipper her, it would have landed on the floor like a dead cat. I showed her a good time. What's wrong with that?

(SELMA returns with mousakka in an elaborate bowl and sets it on table.)

SELMA: Well, here it is!

(Everyone stares and is speechless.)

MANNY: What the hell is that?

SELMA: It's mousakka.

DEBRA: What's in it?

SELMA: All kinds of wonderful things: eggplant, zucchini, tomatoes, beef, pecorino, breadcrumbs—

MANNY: beef and cheese?

SELMA: Yeah.

MANNY: And breadcrumbs?

SELMA: Yes. What's wrong with that?

MANNY: Ma, after hopping up and down all night for a kosher kitchen, what in your right mind possessed you to serve that tref?

SELMA: Oh my goodness. I didn't even realize. I am so sorry. *(She sobs.)* I can't seem to do anything right.

DEBRA: Nice going, Detective Cluseau.

MANNY: What? What? Are we not observing the holiday? You know you've been on my case the entire night. "Don't say this." "Why'd ya say that?"

DEBRA: And everything you have to say, you only tell Marge. What is she the only person here tonight?

MANNY: She's Ma's guest. I'm being nice to her.

DEBRA: Why are you always nice to everyone but me?

MANNY: I am not.

DEBRA: You are too.

MANNY: This is ridiculous. I am not going to put up with this. I'm leaving. Marge, do you want to come with me?

MARGE: No thanks, Manny. I'm good.

DEBRA: See what I mean?

SELMA: This night is a disaster. It couldn't get any worse.

(The doorbell rings.)

MARGE: It's lovely. I'm having the time of my life.

SELMA: You are?

MARGE: Well, no, not really.

(The doorbell rings.)

DEBRA: There's someone at the door.

SELMA: If it's Moshany with more kugel, I'm not interested.

MANNY: I doubt he'd come out on the yuntif. Isn't he religious?

SELMA: Well, who else could it be?

DEBRA: You could answer it and find out.

SELMA: This was supposed to be a special meal. I really had an incredible time in Greece, and I so wanted to share a part of it with everyone.

MARGE: Now, now. It's okay.

(Enter MIKOS.)

MIKOS: I heard voices and door was open.

MANNY: Ma's good on kugel, Moshany.

DEBRA and MARGE: That's not Moshany!

SELMA: Mikos!

DEBRA, MARGE and MANNY: Mikos?

MIKOS: My Beautiful Desdemona!

DEBRA, MARGE, and MANNY: Desdemona?

MIKOS: At long last, it is you!

SELMA: Mikos, what are you doing here?

MARGE: You know him?

MIKOS: Yes, in Greece, in the beautiful island of Mykonos, Desdemona and I explore enjoyment of the palate, fine food, fresh wine, and we partake in Greek delight!

SELMA: Yes, uh, we partake in Greek food! Mikos was very helpful in the Greek market. Weren't you, Mikos? This is my son, Manny and his wife Debra, and my dear friend, Marjorie.

MIKOS: A pleasure to make your acquaintances.

SELMA: Everyone, this is Mikos. This is such a surprise. How did you find me?

MIKOS: American Express, don't leave home without it.

SELMA: My credit card. Come, Mikos, please join us at the table.

MIKOS: Beautiful Desdemona, why do you keep plastic cover over fine tablecloth?

SELMA: Well, life in Hoboken is nothing like in the Greek Isles.

MANNY: Why do you keep calling Mom, Desdemona?

MIKOS: Well when we spoke during her mass—

SELMA: Oh, yes, it's a funny story. Mikos, you know you can call me Selma.

MIKOS: Certainly, beautiful Selma.

DEBRA: Can we get you something to eat?

MIKOS: Ah! I see you prepare my favorite meal, mousakka!

SELMA: Yes! I mean no, no, no.

MANNY: How exactly do you know my mother?

SELMA: Mikos, how about if I make you a plate. Here's some gefilte fish and moussaka.

MIKOS: What kind of fish is the gefilte? In what waters does it swim? *(Everyone is baffled; DEBRA giggles.)*

MARGE: *(Pause)* Were you on the tour together?

MIKOS: No, it was in the beautiful island of Mykonos, when Selma and I partake in two favorite things: mousakka and Greek delight.

MANNY: What's this Greek delight he keeps talking about?

DEBRA: Yeah, and why's it so special?

MARGE: It must be some unique seasoning they put in the food. I'll try the mousakka.

DEBRA: Me too.

MANNY: So, Mikos, aside from eating mousakka and partaking in Greek delight, what else do you do in Mykonos?

MIKOS: I am masseur.

MANNY: You are mister who?

DEBRA: No, not "monsieur"; it's "masseur." He gives massages.

SELMA: *(To MIKOS)* Yes, and they are wonderful.

MANNY: You gave my mother a massage?

MARGE: This is getting interesting. By the way, Selma, I'm having a good time now.

SELMA: Well, after I injured myself, I hobbled along the street and happened to stroll into a Greek—

MANNY: Bathhouse? I've heard about those places.

DEBRA: Me too!

MARGE: Well, I haven't. Will somebody please tell me?

MIKOS: My beloved Selma. How I've longed for your sweet scent, the touch of your skin next to mine, and to again partake in Greek delight!

MANNY: Wait a minute. Did you take advantage of my mother? How could you do that to a widow? And now you've come to our holiday dinner to gloat?

MIKOS: Surely, I did not take advantage and did not come to gloat!

SELMA: True, it was nothing like that.

MANNY: Well, what exactly was it?

MARGE: Yeah, what was it?

DEBRA: Yeah.

SELMA: Well, when I first entered the massage room, I didn't feel comfortable taking off my clothes but then Mikos made me feel welcome –

MANNY: I bet! You want Greek delight? Just wait till you feel the touch of my fist on your face!

DEBRA: No, Manny, don't!

MANNY: Why not?

DEBRA: It's not in the spirit of the holiday!

MANNY: Who is this guy, anyway?

MIKOS: I am Mikos and I have come for my loving and honest Selma. Please return to Greece with me. Together we will explore the beautiful island of Mykonos by day and watch rapturous sunsets by night.

SELMA: Mikos, dear Mikos. That is so lovely, and I am so truly touched.

MIKOS: Then you will return with me. It is settled.

MANNY: Wait a minute! Are you out of your mind or is your head full of grape leaves? She's not going anywhere, and certainly not with you.

SELMA: Manny, let me handle it. Mikos, I can't go back with you.

MARGE: Why not? Are you crazy?

DEBRA: Yeah, you should go with him!

MIKOS: Why can you not return with me, my sweet Selma?

SELMA: Mikos, you are wonderful and I so enjoyed our time in Mykonos. And this experience has brought something out in me that I didn't know was there anymore or ever would be. I feel alive again. I will always remember you for that. From the bottom of my heart, thank you Mikos.

MIKOS: You are welcome, my beautiful Selma, and you are always welcome in Mykonos.

SELMA: And if you are ever again in Hoboken, you are welcome. I think you should go now. I'll walk you to the door.

MIKOS: Of course. Here is something you left in Mykonos. *(He takes out pebble and hands to SELMA.)* Forgive me for intruding on family holiday. At age of fourteen, my mother, Agatha, die and I work all trades to feed young sister and brother. Please enjoy precious time with loving mother and family.

MANNY: Mikos, please stay and enjoy the rest of the dinner with us. I insist.

SELMA: That's a wonderful idea.

EVERYONE: Dai dai anu, dai dai anu, dai dai anu, dai anu dai anu, daianu.

SCENE V

(Tombstone of Sol Steinhart.)

SELMA: My beloved Sol. Thanks for giving me your okay. That was some trip to Greece! I'm sorry we couldn't walk hand-in-hand as we had always hoped, but I saw your face at every bookshop, museum and café. I hope it's alright, and I don't want to upset you, but I won't be able to visit like before.

I've decided it's my time to move out of the undefined gray and back into the circle. Wish me luck on this journey, my love. *(She removes pebble from pocket and places on tombstone.)* Until we meet again.

(Lights fade to black.)
(The End)

MI MEDIA NARANJA

By Rolls Andre

Rolls Andre holds an MFA in Acting from the National Theatre Conservatory and a BFA in Theatre from Florida International University. He is an English teacher living in Brooklyn, New York. This is his first play.

Mi Media Naranja made its New York City debut on July 28th 2011 at the Hudson Guild Theatre. It was a semi-finalist in The Riant Theatre's Summer 2011 Strawberry One-Act Festival with the following cast, in order of appearance:

MARCUS	Rolls Andre
REGGIE	Kim Gainer
ARLEEN	Jen Taher

The play was directed by Lauren Moran Mills.

CAST OF CHARACTERS
MARCUS, an overweight black man in his late thirties.
REGGIE, an attractive black woman in her mid-thirties.
ARLEEN, Super freak.

(At rise, MARCUS JORDAN, is seated at the table pouring himself a whiskey. He is in his pajamas and appears agitated. REGGIE JORDAN, dressed in a short night gown and kimono enters and looks at him incredulously. After a moment or two she speaks.)

REGGIE: What's going on? You were only in there for like five minutes.

MARCUS: I need another drink.

REGGIE: Do you think that's a good idea?

MARCUS: I'm a grown man, Reggie. *(He makes himself a drink and downs it in one. He pours another.)*

REGGIE: It's just —

MARCUS: What?!? *(He downs his drink and pours another.)*

REGGIE: Lower your voice! You'll wake Dontay! You need to stay focused.

MARCUS: Dat's what you say!

REGGIE: *(She pulls the bottle out of his grasp.)* You are 86ed! Get in that bedroom. Now.

MARCUS: I can't.

REGGIE: Marcus we talked about this!

MARCUS: No, you talked and as usual I swallowed my rage in silence.

REGGIE: Get in there.

MARCUS: I'm telling you I can't. This is on you. You brought her here to begin with.

REGGIE: But you're the one that killed her. *(She goes over and makes herself a drink. She looks at MARCUS and pours him one too. She brings it to him.)* Bottoms up baby. We've been over this and over this. It's the only way.

MARCUS: This is crazy Reggie. We gotta call the police.

REGGIE: So what happens after you do the right thing Spike? I'll tell you: our lives become more fucked than your mother on nickel night! You listen to me Marcus Jordan. I got you the garbage bags and my sharpest most expensive kitchen knife and cleaver. I even helped you get her in the tub. Now you gotta get her out. Piece by piece.

MARCUS: Goddamnit woman…that's a real person in there!

REGGIE: A person you killed. I know!

MARCUS: I DIDN'T KILL HER!

REGGIE: Don't wake the baby! All I know, one minute we're all fucking and sucking there she is: Live skank. I go to the bathroom for two minutes. Two itty bitty minutes so I could gargle and floss. And when I come back there she is: Deceased skank. Somebody killed the shit out that bitch and it wasn't me.

MARCUS: She died okay? Nobody killed anybody! Why do you keep saying that?

REGGIE: Because that's what the police will say. And the neighbors. And Daddy. My God if he finds out…we can't let that happen.

MARCUS: Fuck "Old Oil Spill."

REGGIE: You watch your mouth.

MARCUS: Your father's blacker than a cloud of coal dust and you know it.

REGGIE: He pays your salary so don't you insult my father.

MARCUS: You just called my mother a 'ho. And a reasonably priced one at that!

REGGIE: Focus Marcus. I'm sure a proper investigation will show that this is nothing more than a horrible accident.

MARCUS: Right. That's all this is.

REGGIE: As I said, I'm sure a proper investigation will show that. But that's when our problems begin. Said investigation would shed light on areas of our lives I'd prefer to keep shady. Understand?

MARCUS: Of course—

REGGIE: Really? Our neighbors and families, your co-workers would know about us and how we have chosen to live. They would judge us. Condemn us. Laugh at us. The authorities might deem us unfit and take away our son.

MARCUS: Jesus.

REGGIE: Yeah. This is just some run of the mill bar skank baby. Low lifes like her end up dismembered in garbage bags every day. But we're good people who pay taxes, have mortgages, raise families…think about your son for godsakes. I am not going to have my life ripped away from me because of some stupid accident. So are you gonna go do your manly duty and chop her up or should I go get a bottle of Kikoman so you can just eat her instead?

MARCUS: Great just what we need right now: fat jokes.

REGGIE: Who's joking Marcus? When you lay on your side in bed I can't get a signal on my cell phone! (*Silence. MARCUS goes to the bottle and pours another.*)

MARCUS: Where did you dig up that knickknack anyway?

REGGIE: Was there a problem?

MARCUS: You mean besides the fact that her vagina looked like Walter Matthau frowning?

REGGIE: You were balls deep in that "knickknack" before she took her clothes off.

MARCUS: I gotta get up to get to work by 8AM sharp so I can let your father violate my soul hole.

REGGIE: You seemed pretty damned into her to me. Why don't you get into me like that anymore?

MARCUS: Reggie please- this is not a Wednesday at 3:37 AM kinda conversation—

REGGIE: You won't touch me…now you won't even talk to me. I just wanted to fuck my husband for the first time in months. I'm sorry.

MARCUS: (*With vehemence.*) We talked about this.

REGGIE: No you talked and as usual I pretended to give a shit.

MARCUS: We agreed that our days of swinging are over now. We had our fun, but now we have a son. We have to be more responsible.

REGGIE: What's so responsible about eating birthday cake for breakfast?

MARCUS: Enough!

REGGIE: Why don't you ever say that about gravy? *(Beat)* Why are you trying to kill yourself?!?

MARCUS: What do I have to live for?

REGGIE: What did you say?

MARCUS: After 8-12 hours a day with your father where I'm left all broken and bloody like Cissy Spacek in the locker room scene in *Carrie*, I gotta come back here and clock in for the night shift so you can use my dreams for your tampons! Yeah some life I got.

REGGIE: Do you even love me anymore? *(They pause for an awkward beat. MARCUS pulls a candy bar out of his pocket. She slaps it out of his hand.)* Marcus Jordan, do you love me or not? Answer me!

MARCUS: *(Beat)* Don't make me say it…. *(REGGIE turns her back and walks away perhaps to hide her tears.)*

REGGIE: I did everything for you. I loved you. Loved you enough to let other people into our bed. It terrified me at first but I learned to love that danger. Learned to live for it. Almost as much as I lived for you. And just because you asked me to. Because I wanted to make a life with you. *(Silence.)*

MARCUS: *(Suppressing a yawn.)* Look can we just call the police now? Please?

REGGIE: What do you have to complain about Marcus? You don't hear me bitching that all I do with my life is spend all day everyday with Duh-duh-duh-Dontay!

MARCUS: Regina Liggins Jordan!

REGGIE: I love him with all my heart but you know as well as I do that he doesn't have the brains God gave a potato. Or the looks. He looks like what would happen if scientists learned to successfully mate a monkey with a hunk of shit.

MARCUS: You're his mother! You know that right?

REGGIE: I know…and I feel….so sorry for him. Poor little Dontay… what kinda monsters are we? What kinda hell on earth have we made for him? When it's his bath time I don't know whether to put him in the tub or flush him down the toilet.

MARCUS: There are no words.

REGGIE: I knew we weren't getting things quite right lately but I thought we were in this together. That we were both fighting to keep this thing alive. I was wrong huh?

MARCUS: As wrong as wearing socks with sandals. *(They sit in silence for a moment or so.)*

REGGIE: Just for the record….this is still about dat white bitch right?

MARCUS: Tread lightly Reggie. I don't need two dead skanks up in here.

REGGIE: Excuse me for not having anything nice to say about some bitch who fucked my husband.

MARCUS: I fucked mad bitches right in front of you.

REGGIE: Out in the open! Always! And you shared said bitches with me. But with Debbie Solomon you got all greedy and broke the rules. You know I can't allow that!

MARCUS: Don't…say…her name…ever…

REGGIE: Goddamn, what did she do to you Marcus? What was her secret besides not being me?

MARCUS: I could have lived in her lap. You have no idea what you stole from me!

REGGIE: She was never yours! Ever. Because she never knew who you really were. You lied to her. You can't say you love someone and lie to them!

MARCUS: I would have told her. I was going to tell her.

REGGIE: You're kidding yourself. No way would she have stayed here in town if she knew. You should have seen her face when I told her. My God… she looked like she didn't know whether to cry or to vomit. Like she had just seen Santa Claus getting gang raped.

MARCUS: *(Beat)* Why?

REGGIE: Because I love you! I thought if she was gone maybe we could get back to us. Like it used to be. Before Dontay. But now I see I fucked up okay? I admit it. And I want you to know that I am sorry. I never meant to hurt you like this. You don't know how much I wish I could go back and let her have you. That's how much I love you. I'd rather you be happy with her than miserable and morbidly obese with me. Doesn't that mean anything to you?

MARCUS: You are a spoiled, needy, hard headed cunt. And a lying sack of shit with a princess complex to boot. Your selfish ass couldn't stand letting another little girl play with one of your dollies. Well you can lie to yourself if you want but let me tell you this: I AM TIRED OF YOU PISSING IN MY MOUF AND TELLING ME IT'S LEMONADE!

(And with that DONTAY starts to howling! The two of them look at each other to see who'll go get him. Neither moves a muscle. After a moment, miracle of miracles, the baby stops crying. They go back to ignoring each other. After a while,

ARLEEN comes out of the bedroom holding Dontay, who is all swaddled. She is a white woman in her 30's? It's hard to tell because she has seen some significant wear and tear. She has partied way too much for way too long and shows signs of decay. Her hair and makeup is a mess. Her clothes are tacky and torn.)

ARLEEN: Hey keep it down. You woke up the little lawn jockey. *(Silence. REGGIE and MARCUS stare at ARLEEN.)* Ssshhh…what's his name?

REGGIE: Dontay.

ARLEEN: Cute. Shhh… Dontay. Ssshhhh….. *(She starts to sing him something in the public domain. After a moment:)* How old is he?

REGGIE: 5…no 6 months.

ARLEEN: Oh, I got a little girl named Sasha about your age back home.

MARCUS: You have a child?

ARLEEN: Children. 7 of 'em.

REGGIE: *(Whispering to MARCUS)* That explains why it looks like a Picasso in her underpants.

ARLEEN: Yep. Sasha, Jason, Jenny, Conner, Greg, Dylan and Masoud. And don't go jumping to any conclusions either. They all got the same Father. Mine.

MARCUS: I'm sorry?

ARLEEN: *(Punching him in the arm. Hard.)* I'm playing with you Cleveland. I ain't got no kids…sometimes I like to pretend tho'. Dreaming about those cute lil fetal a'cohol syndrome faces…smiling at me…the Chlamydia Daddy gave me when I was twelve made me all sterile and whatnot.

REGGIE: Can I have my baby back now?

ARLEEN: *(Handing REGGIE the baby after a moment.)* Of course…here ya go. *(She sits and pours herself a whiskey and drains it.)*

MARCUS: In light of the tragic and unspeakable scenario you disclosed to us just now…I urge you not to take what I am about to say in a negative way. But…you see…we were getting "adjusted" to the idea of you being deceased. I myself was embracing it body and soul in fact.

ARLEEN: My fault. Yeah that happens sometimes. I got some health issues or some shit. *(She takes a drag off her cig and coughs violently.)* What. Ever. Lucky I came to before you started cutting me up. *(She rubs her thigh.)* I wasn't so lucky the last time.

REGGIE: This has happened to you before?

ARLEEN: Just last week I came to nekkid in the Bronx with a hare lipped Dominican named Felix using my mouth as an ashtray.

MARCUS: Jesus.

ARLEEN: That's right his brother Jesus was there too. Jacking off in the corner.

REGGIE: Could you…umm…stop talking? You're making me queasy.

ARLEEN: Listen to Princess Di over there. Sorry your highness. I've seen some shit in my time. I once seent a rat give a hooker CPR.

MARCUS: You lyin'!

ARLEEN: Saved her muthafuckin' life. Stupid bitch died a few months later though from the rabies.

REGGIE: SHUT UP!

ARLEEN: Well excuse me Miss Priss. Maybe I should be going?

MARCUS: Maybe that's for the best. This has been some day. Simply endless. You need some cash or anything?

ARLEEN: *(Heated.)* I ain't no goddamned concubine ya heard? *(She pounces on MARCUS.)* You took my privates to Pound Town you, big black animal. *(To REGGIE)* You must be a pretty amazing lady to deserve some dick like this here.

REGGIE: Thank you for recognizing, unlike some others around here, that I am indeed a rare and precious jewel that shines out of any setting. Now please get the fuck out of my house.

ARLEEN: *(Rubbing her tummy)* You mind if I clock in at the fudge factory and do some important paperwork firs'? *(REGGIE is about to object.)*

MARCUS: That's fine uh —

ARLEEN: Arleen.

MARCUS: Oh I thought you said *Marlene* earlier. Hard to tell what with my dick all in your mouth. *(They both laugh.)* I'm Marcus. *(REGGIE clears her throat loudly.)*

MARCUS: Well okay Arleen, it's late and I still need to give Reggie her heartworm medicine.

ARLEEN: Good one Benson. God you two sure are lucky.

MARCUS: Oh yeah? Why's that?

ARLEEN: Your beautiful kid. This beautiful house. The fact that you both found your "media naranja."

MARCUS: "Media naranja" what's that?

REGGIE: Yeah we don't speak "housekeeper."

ARLEEN: "Mi media naranja" it means "my other half." It's what you call the person who loves you like no one else can love you and needs you like no one else can need you. I mean I love feeling like a feather in a whirlwind – I really do – I don't know nothing else – but sometimes I think it would be nice to have roots like you two and find "Mi media naranja." *(She sighs. She suddenly doubles over as if in pain.)* Ooooh gotta float a meat loaf. Stupid Crohn's. *(She exits to the toilet. MARCUS crosses to the table and sits.)*

REGGIE: Marcus —

MARCUS: Not another word.

REGGIE: But —

MARCUS: Seriously, if you don't want me to disappear into the night with "Little Miss Feather in a Whirlwind," you will let me eat my fish sandwich in peace.

REGGIE: Fish sandwich? *(He reaches into the bowl of fruit on the table and pulls out said sandwich. It is unwrapped.)*

MARCUS: Ta da.

REGGIE: *(Trailing off.)* Aaah....yes....I thought I smelled something....

MARCUS: *(With real feeling.)* Mi media naranja.....
(He begins to eat the sandwich as the lights fade to black....)

(The End)

Kathryn Neville Brown *as MARY* and Steve Hauck *as HARRY*
in BIRD WATCHING by Jeffrey L. Hollman

BIRD WATCHING

By Jeffrey L. Hollman

Jeffrey L. Hollman spent thirty five years in education as an English teacher, Assistant Principal, High School Principal, and Assistant Superintendent before retiring to write full time. Two of his plays REAL DANGER and FOR THE GOOD OF THE NATION were produced Off-Off Broadway by the Emerging Artists Theatre Company, and BIRD WATCHING was produced by the Riant Theatre.

BIRD WATCHING made its debut at the Strawberry One-Act Festival on August 16, 2009 at the Theatre at St. Clements in Manhattan. It was a finalist in The Riant Theatre's 2009 Strawberry One-Act Festival with the following cast, in order of appearance:

HARRY	Steve Hauck
MARY	Kathryn Neville Browne
LARRY (Lawrence)	Rich Hollman
WOMAN'S VOICE	Kathryn Neville Browne

The play was directed by Jeffrey L. Hollman.

CAST OF CHARACTERS

HARRY: Forties. Camel hair topcoat, brown leather gloves, Russian fur hat.
MARY: Forties. Black high heels, red coat, black gloves, well-groomed hair, black leather pocketbook.

LARRY (Lawrence): Young, handsome. Enthusiastic and boyish. Tan LL Bean hiking coat, jeans, knit wool hat with ears and ties, binoculars, <u>Peterson Field Guide to Eastern Birds</u> sticking out of pocket. Other than the hat, which makes him look goofy, he is handsome and appealing.

WOMAN'S VOICE (WV) from Offstage: LARRY'S bird-watching partner. Heard, not seen. Played by the actor playing MARY.

TIME & SETTING: *(It is a little before noon on a late winter/early spring Saturday in Central Park, New York City. Park bench and a wire trash basket. Some winter trees and bushes.)*

AT RISE: *(Arm in arm, HARRY and MARY enter from SL. They stop to kiss deeply.)*

HARRY: *(Pulls back without letting her go.)* You have a little time. Let's sit here a minute.

MARY: *(Looks at watch.)* K. *(She looks out over the audience, the lake.)* It's nice here. Look at the color of that water.

HARRY: Yeah. *(Pause)* I have a thought.

MARY: What?

HARRY: Skip the appointment. Let's go back to the hotel.

MARY: You could go for more? Already? That's amaz—

HARRY: It's you. Nobody has ever—look, skip the appointment.

MARY: I can't—

HARRY: I paid for the room till two.

MARY: Harry, I can't. It's why I came into the city.

HARRY: I thought you came to see me.

MARY: Oh, I did.

HARRY: So? Skip the appointment. Anyway, who would know?

MARY: Dr. Bernard, for one.

HARRY: Call him, Mary. Say you're sick or stuck in traffic.

MARY: No, his office would call the house.

HARRY: Yeah, but if you call first then—

MARY: Don't...tempt me.

(She kisses him. He returns the kiss, which gets more passionate then stops to crane his neck around making sure no one is nearby. He removes his left hand glove with his teeth because his right arm is behind her back, grinning at her as he does so. He slips the ungloved hand under her coat and between her legs.)

MARY: *(After a moment, she stops his hand.)* Be careful—*(Holds up the glove he has stripped off.)*—you're not wearing protection.

HARRY: *(Chuckles.)* Throw care to the winds! *(Tries to kiss her again, but she pulls back.)* What?

MARY: Would you mind taking off your hat?

HARRY: *(Takes off Russian fur hat and holds it out in front of him.)* What's wrong with my hat?

MARY: I keep thinking it's going to bite me.

HARRY: *(Looking at it proudly.)* Very fashionable in Moscow. Everybody wears one.

MARY: So you've told me.

HARRY: *(Still looking at it.)* Yeah. I told you where I got—

MARY: Yes.

HARRY: Right. And it's really warm.

MARY: It doesn't look like a hat. More like you just coiled an animal on your head.

HARRY: *(Chuckles.)* Maybe that's why I like it. Kind of elemental. *(Mock growl.)* A throwback to an earlier age when men killed animals for food and vestment.

MARY: Well, that creature doesn't look like it's been killed yet. *(Looks at watch.)* Ooo. Have to go. *(Stands.)*

HARRY: *(Stands but does not put his hat back on.)* OK. If you insist. I'll wait for you here.

MARY: I won't be long. Dr. Bernard is very on time...for a doctor... shouldn't be more than a half hour. We'll be able to get coffee before my train.

HARRY: What time is that?

MARY: A little before two.

HARRY: That early?

MARY: I have to. It's an hour on the train then a half hour to my house.

HARRY: Listen. *(Takes hold of her sleeve.)* Go later. Take a later train. We'll go back to the hotel, I'll rent the room for another night, and you—

MARY: I can't stay over night.

HARRY: Neither can I. I have to be home by six. But we'll have the room for the afternoon. You can leave later—four or five o'clock.

MARY: Oh...I would love that. But—

HARRY: Say you went to the Metropolitan. It's right over there. Say you went to the museum after your doctor's appointment and just took a later train.

MARY: *(She looks off in the direction of the museum. Nods her head.)* I've actually done that before. OK. *(Turns back.)* I'll be back in half an hour.

HARRY: I'll be here.

(They kiss then she exits SR. HARRY watches her go then puts his hat back on. Looks at his watch then sits back on the bench. Takes out his Blackberry and just

begins clicking through items when he hears LARRY and the WOMAN talking SR.)

LARRY: *(Offstage.)* Ooo—look—in that birch tree—tufted titmouse!

WOMAN'S VOICE: *(Offstage.)* Where? Ah, yes! *(Pause.)* That's the first titmouse I've seen this spring.

LARRY: *(Offstage.)* Really? They don't migrate. They're here all year round.

WV: *(Offstage.)* Well, I haven't seen one. Plenty of chickadees and nuthatches. And downies. But no titmice.

LARRY: *(Backing onstage from R. Facing away from HARRY on the bench looking up into the trees with his binoculars.)* Sure you have. We saw a whole bunch of titmice last weekend. Over in the Ramble.

WV: *(Offstage.)* I didn't go into The Ramble. Remember? Morry and I went the other way. Around the turtle pond.

LARRY: Oh, that's right.

WV: *(Offstage.)* That's where we saw the surf scoter.

LARRY: *(Still looking up into the trees.)* Right. *(Lowers the binoculars to look off SR to speak to her.)* By the way, are you sure it was a surf scoter? That's an ocean duck.

WV: *(Offstage.)* Morry showed me a picture in the book.

LARRY: *(Raising the binoculars to look up into the trees again.)* Very strange, an ocean duck in a fresh water pond.

WV: *(Offstage. Excited.)* Oh, look! There, at the water's edge. Dark. *(LARRY adjusts his binoculars down SR.)* About twelve inches long. A blue sheen on the black feathers. Long, almost de-curved bill. Yellow—

LARRY: Yeah. *(Looking up again.)* It's a grackle.

WV: *(Offstage.)* You sure it's not a red-wing?

LARRY: *(Looking up into the trees.)* Uh-uh, definitely a grackle. We could see a red-wing today, although it's early. But that's a grackle. *(Without taking his binoculars down.)* Hey, I have an idea. You go that way around the lake, and I'll go this way. We'll meet on the other side and compare notes.

WV: *(Offstage.)* Oh, good idea.

LARRY: *(Takes his binoculars down to look SR to speak to the WOMAN.)* Keep your eyes open for Great Blue Herons. They should be back any day now.

WV: *(Offstage.)* I will.

LARRY: And if you see one, take a close look at the plumes on the breast. I have an idea that they return from down south ready to do their mating display, even this early in the year. *(Lifts his binoculars and looks into the trees SR again.)*

WV: I will. See you on the other side.

LARRY: *(Lowers his binoculars and calls off SR.)* And I'll have more than you by then.

WV: *(Offstage.)* Ha! Challenge accepted!

(LARRY raises his binoculars to look up into the trees again. HARRY watches, a slight smile on his face. LARRY slowly pans through the trees until he is aimed over HARRY'S head. He brings the binoculars lower until they are aimed at HARRY'S hat.)

LARRY: Oh. *(Lowers glasses to look at HARRY.)* I couldn't tell what that was.

HARRY: What?

LARRY: Your hat. *(Approaching and examining the hat.)* That's really something. Wow. I really like that.

HARRY: *(Looks at his Blackberry.)* Well, thanks.

LARRY: *(Looks up into the trees with his binoculars but then takes them down.)* You know, I haven't seen a lot of Russian hats like that in New York.

HARRY: *(Looks up.)* Yeah? *(Looks down again.)*

LARRY: Yeah. Really unique. *(Looks up into the trees again.)* Such a good look.

HARRY: Thanks.

LARRY: *(Takes binoculars down.)* Betcha it's warm, too.

HARRY: *(Looks up.)* Well, there's nothing like real fur.

LARRY: I'll bet. Is that Muskrat?

HARRY: Siberian beaver.

LARRY: Wow. Is it hot? You know, to wear. Is your head hot?

HARRY: No. It breathes. I'm quite comfortable. *(Goes back to Blackberry.)*

LARRY: Hmm. You buy that here...in New York? I'd love to get one. *(Pulls an ear of his hat out and holds it.)* Would be better than this stupid thing when I go birding in winter.

HARRY: *(Looks up at the hat LARRY is wearing.)* No, I got this in Moscow.

LARRY: *(Jerks his binoculars up and leaps SL because he has seen a bird in the trees above. Looks a moment.)* Aa. Just a flicker. *(Lowers glasses and turns back to HARRY who has watched him leap about looking for the flicker.)* On vacation?

HARRY: What?

LARRY: Were you on vacation? In Moscow?

HARRY: Oh, no, I go regularly. Business.

LARRY: Must be a lot of stores selling these babies there, huh?

HARRY: There are. But this was a gift.

LARRY: Oh—

HARRY: From Vladimir Putin.

LARRY: No-o-o. Get outa here. The President of Russia? That Vladimir Putin?

HARRY: Yup.

LARRY: The President of Russia gave you this hat? How come? What'd you do?

HARRY: I work for a consortium that's building a gas pipeline into Eastern Europe from Russia.

LARRY: *(Looks up into the trees with his binoculars.)* What? For Gazprom?

HARRY: That's right. You know about that?

LARRY: Sure. That's a big deal. *(Lowers the binoculars.)* That's the company Putin stole, right?

HARRY: No-o-o. He didn't steal it—

LARRY: Well, who cares? You met Putin. Sat down with Vladimir Putin, the Russian President, and signed contracts. And he gave you this hat.

HARRY: Well, he gave a hat to each of us at a ceremony. *(During this, LARRY looks up through his binoculars again.)* I didn't actually sit down to sign papers with him. They were already signed. Previously. You know, before the ceremony.

LARRY: Ah. *(Pause as he looks through binoculars.)* How many hats did he give out?

HARRY: Hell, I don't know.

LARRY: Two?

HARRY: No. No, more than that.

LARRY: Three?

HARRY: No, a lot more than that.

LARRY: *(Lowers his binoculars and looks at HARRY.)* What? Like fifty?

HARRY: Not sure. Maybe.

LARRY: Fifty fur hats? What did you do, line up to get them?

HARRY: *(Laughs.)* No. They were at our places at the banquet table. In boxes.

LARRY: Oh. So it wasn't like Putin went into a store to buy that hat for you.

HARRY: *(Chuckles.)* No. No, he didn't personally go buy this hat for me.

LARRY: Oh. *(LARRY stares at HARRY.)* It kinda sounded that way.

HARRY: Well, no, I don't think I really.... *(LARRY continues to stare. To break the silence.)* What's a TITmouse?

LARRY: What? Oh. *(Holds his binoculars out.)* A little bird.

HARRY: No-o-o. I thought it was a little grey rodent with big boobs.

LARRY: What?

HARRY: Just kidding. I know it's a bird. I mean, that is what you're doing, right? Bird watching? I was just asking what kind.

LARRY: It's called a tufted titmouse because he has a little crest—or tuft—on his head.

HARRY: But why tit-mouse? Who ever came up with a name for a little bird that combines a female body part with a type of rodent?

LARRY: I've never even thought of that before. Huh. It's always just been a titmouse to me. I don't know what its derivation is. *(Thinks.)* Female body part with a rodent. That's...really...wow.

HARRY: I mean, is there a bird called a...I don't know...a vagina rat?

LARRY: Oh, my god! A vagin—I can't even say that.

HARRY: Sorry, friend, but I couldn't believe you were telling that woman there she was looking at a TIT-mouse.

LARRY: Really? Hmm. *(Looks up into the trees overhead with his binoculars. HARRY just watches him a moment then goes back to his Blackberry. LARRY lowers his binoculars.)* Well...I'll be off

HARRY: *(Looks up.)* OK. Good hunting.

(LARRY exits SL. HARRY resumes looking at his Blackberry for several seconds. LARRY re-enters from SL and walks directly to the bench and sits on the other end from HARRY who looks up from the Blackberry.)

LARRY: That's really amazing. What you just did.

HARRY: What?

LARRY: You've changed how I will think about that bird forever.

HARRY: The titmouse?

LARRY: I almost can't say it now. Yes. The titmouse.

HARRY: And...is that—?

LARRY: Yes.

HARRY: Yes...what?

LARRY: It is bad.

HARRY: It's just a bird. It's just the name of a bird.

LARRY: It's not that simple. You have to understand. I have known about the tufted titmouse...well...all my life.

HARRY: I said I was sorry.

LARRY: That doesn't change the effect, though...the damage.

HARRY: Damage?

LARRY: It's one of my earliest memories.

HARRY: Look, I'm—

LARRY: Don't you have a memory that's...like...very important—no, precious—to you?

HARRY: Precious?

LARRY: My father had one of these little clear plastic bird feeders that he attached to a picture window with little suction cups, and I used to sit right by the window as birds came to take sunflower seeds. I was very little, maybe four or five.

HARRY: Look, I can see that—

LARRY: Black-capped chickadees...house finches...occasionally nut-hatches...and tufted titmice perched two inches from my nose, so close that I could see individual feathers, their toenails, even their eyelids. *(Turns to look at HARRY.)* My Dad and I would make little cards for each bird we saw and keep them in the pages of the bird book.

HARRY: Well, that sounds very—

LARRY: I still remember the surprise I felt at seeing all those colors. Most people see a bird and think they are just little grey balls of feather, but when you really look closely, you see so much pattern, so many shades of color. Take sparrows—

HARRY: *(Calmly.)* No, you take them. I'm sorry, friend, but I don't have time for this. I apologize for unwittingly altering your past, but it was just that. Unwitting. I did not do it on purpose. Now, I'd like to just sit here and go through my calls and notes. *(Holds up Blackberry).*

LARRY: *(Nods his head.)* Do you really mean that?

HARRY: Yes, I just want to go through my calls and—

LARRY: No, no. I mean are you really sorry for altering my past?

HARRY: God. Yes. If I could take it back, I would. If there was something I could do to change it, I would do that for you. But I can't, and so I would like it very much—

(During this last, LARRY begins looking intently out over the audience, the lake. Suddenly jumps up and runs DS to look out over the audience. Cups his ear.)

LARRY: WHAT? *(Listens cupping his ears then forms a megaphone with his hands.)* I CAN'T HEAR YOU. *(Cups his ears again and listens.)* WAIT TILL WE MEET UP. *(Turns back to HARRY.)* Could you hear what she was saying?

HARRY: No. Now please go away. Go compare notes with your friend. You can tell her how I destroyed your childhood. Tell her how I called your precious titmouse a vagina rat and forever ruined the relationship you had with your father.

LARRY: Whoa. How did you get to all that?

HARRY: Leave—me—alone.

LARRY: I will. But you're really—I don't know—Who said anything about ruining?—

HARRY: *(Getting up.)* Good bye.

LARRY: No. No. Don't. I'll go. Don't you go. *(Stands and goes off SL.*

HARRY sits back down then after a long moment LARRY re-renters and stands just onstage. Speaks earnestly. HARRY looks up annoyed.) I'm sorry. I can tell you're a good man and weren't looking to hurt anyone. It was just my reaction. I am sorry.

HARRY: I thought you were leaving.

LARRY: Yeah. OK. *(Turns away then back.)* Before I go, I just want to say one thing. You know, I never expected this. It's funny, I came to the park to track the birds that are returning from their winter ranges, but I end up arguing with a complete stranger instead. I can see how you could question such a name. Titmouse. It is weird. I just never thought about it before. I was just a little shocked and, I guess—I really am sorry. *(HARRY looks up from his Blackberry.)* Please. Accept my apology.

HARRY: OK. Yeah, I do.

LARRY: God. I can't believe I turned myself into one of those annoying strangers you meet on the streets all the time.

HARRY: We just disagreed on something.

LARRY: Like one of those crazy guys who, if you just make eye contact with them, they begin telling you the most unconnected stuff.

HARRY: No-o-o. And...I shouldn't have said anything about your father. I deserved your anger.

LARRY: Really?

HARRY: I was being flip with that comment. *(To himself.)* Good, Harry, minimize it.

LARRY: *(Approaching more closely.)* No, my name's Larry, not Harry. But how would you—?

HARRY: I was talking to myself. *(LARRY just looks at him.)* My name is Harry.

LARRY: Oh.

HARRY: You're Larry?

LARRY: Yeah.

HARRY: *(Chuckle.)* Larry and Harry. Well. Nice to meet you. *(Nods at him.)*

LARRY: Likewise. *(Nods back.)* What did you say? What were you minimizing?

HARRY: OK. *(Thinks.)* Would you mind if I told you something, Larry?

LARRY: About? *(Approaches and sits at the opposite end of the bench.)*

HARRY: Me.

LARRY: Sure. Go ahead.

HARRY: You sure? I don't want you to think I'm one of those people you meet who suddenly begins telling you unconnected, crazy stuff.

LARRY: *(Chuckles.)* No-o-o, you don't seem like that. What were you minimizing?

HARRY: *(Takes a breath.)* OK. I was minimizing when I said I was being flip when I made that joke about the bird's name. Minimizing is a form of dishonesty.

LARRY: How—dishonesty?

HARRY: A moment of apology should be a moment of total honesty. Even to a stranger.

LARRY: OK, but I didn't take it you were being dishonest, Harry. It actually felt pretty good when you said you deserved my anger.

HARRY: That was honest. But saying I was being flip was glossing over what I had done. I was nasty to you and should have been earnest in my apology. But, no, I was flip. I glossed over. Glossing over is a form of dishonesty.

LARRY: You've been talking to someone, huh?

HARRY: Huh?

LARRY: A therapist? Oh, I shouldn't have asked you that.

HARRY: No, that's OK. But what makes you say that?

LARRY: Well...please, don't take this wrong, but what you were saying sounded a little like...jargon. "Glossing over?"

HARRY: *(Not a laugh.)* Ha.

LARRY: Like you were repeating something a therapist would say—unless you got it from some self-help book.

HARRY: No. *(Shakes his head quickly like in disgust.)* No, I am seeing a shrink. LARRY: Psychiatrist?

HARRY: See? I did it again. I minimized by calling my therapist a shrink. Made the classic joke out of it.

LARRY: You really are too hard on yourself.

HARRY: Well—

LARRY: I'm seeing a shrink, too, and I don't mind calling him that. Actually, I have other names for him, as well.

HARRY: You're not happy with him?

LARRY: Hell, no. Doesn't say a word, this guy. I would love to quote some jargon back at you, but this guy doesn't say anything. Barely nods at me.

HARRY: Doesn't say anything? That help?

LARRY: Now that's the question. He's a FROY-DEE-EN. Doesn't even say hi when I come in. I'm going to quit. My mother wants me to see him. He's useless.

HARRY: Sounds like—

LARRY: I've joined a meditation group, and frankly I get more out of that. *(Pause.)* Yours talks?

HARRY: Too much. Sometimes I feel like I hardly get a word in edgewise and then she says, "It looks like we're at the end of our hour."

LARRY: Ha! Forty five minutes, you mean.

HARRY: You know, you're right. I didn't realize that for the first several sessions. She charges two hundred and fifty bucks *an hour* but always ends after forty five minutes.

LARRY: At least you walk away having actually heard something for your money. *(Pause.)* So you're seeing her because you think you're dishonest?

HARRY: Well...in part...yeah.

LARRY: You think that things like—as you call it—being flip make you dishonest?

HARRY: It's part of a pattern. A better example is this hat. *(Takes the hat off and looks at it. Nods solemnly.)* This is a perfect example—not just with you but with anyone else who sees me with this on my head. The ceremony was in a room so big that I could hardly see Putin. Somebody actually had to point him out to me when he entered the hall and walked to the head table. One bald headed guy among scores of other bald headed guys. I probably got no closer to him than a hundred yards.

LARRY: Wow. Big room, huh?

HARRY: Oh, it was huge. But when the subject of this hat comes up— and I am almost always the one to bring it up—I tell people Vladimir Putin gave it to me. *(Tosses the hat in the trash container.)* I'm throwing it out. *(Reaches back in and takes the hat out to offer it to LARRY.)* No. You liked it, you take it.

LARRY: You really are too critical of yourself. I mean, you were there, in a room with Putin—

HARRY: A very big room. *(Tosses hat on the bench where it remains.)*

LARRY: OK, but you've seen him in person regardless of distance. I've only seen him on TV...or in a newspaper.

HARRY: Yeah, but why do I have to phrase it like Vladimir and I were kicking back shots of vodka together and then he gave me his hat?

LARRY: You didn't do that. You didn't say he gave you *his* hat.

HARRY: No, but I make it sound that way. Take this morning. I was telling a friend about this hat and made it sound like Putin actually placed it in my hands.

LARRY: That the lady in the red coat?

HARRY: You saw her?

LARRY: Sure. She was easy to see. Especially with binoculars. *(Holds them up.)*

HARRY: Where were you?

LARRY: *(Points offstage R.)* Over there. With my friend. I was looking around when I caught a bit of red through the branches.

HARRY: You could see us?

LARRY: Only her. I thought she was alone. I didn't see you until I walked over here.

HARRY: No?

LARRY: No. You blend in. It's funny. Humans—for the most part—are the opposite of the birds—for the most part.

HARRY: How's that?

LARRY: Well, with humans, it's the female that wears the brighter—or more decorative—covering. Like your lady friend. With birds, it's the male. You know, a male cardinal is bright red—like your friend—and the female is more drab. Like you. Not that you don't look fashionable.

HARRY*: (Chuckles.)* Gee, thanks. New clothing style: drab fashionable.

LARRY: *(Chuckles.)* Sorry. Not drab. I mean you blend in.

HARRY: You're pretty serious about birds, huh?

LARRY: Yeah. Actually, I'm getting a masters degree in ornithology. At Cornell.

HARRY: Cornell, huh? Yeah, you seem like a pretty smart guy.

LARRY: Thanks. Yeah, I've always loved birds. I've never been interested in anything else. There's nothing like them. Everybody thinks the dinosaurs became extinct, but they didn't. They became birds. They exist everywhere, in every kind of habitat. Their behaviors are fascinating, they're beautiful. And they occupy the air.

HARRY: But what can you do with a degree in ornithology?

LARRY: I really want to do field research. I want to go places few humans have ever stepped foot and find new species. That's what I really want to do. But I'll probably end up teaching.

HARRY: It's really nice to see such enthusiasm in a young man.

LARRY: Yeah. My mother's not crazy about it, but...well, she's OK with it now...sort of.

HARRY: What does she want you to be?

LARRY: Oh, you know, doctor or lawyer...or go into business.

HARRY: What about your dad?

LARRY: He doesn't say much about it...but he's the reason I'm studying birds.

HARRY: Your dad.

LARRY: Yeah. I told you about the cards we kept on the birds we spotted. He also took me out in the woods a lot when I was little. First time I saw a great blue heron was with him. *(Pause.)* Dad said that bird watching satisfied the urge to hunt. We are killers by nature, he would say.

HARRY: And does it do that for you?

LARRY: I've thought about it a lot, but…well I'm not sure it satisfies some urge to kill, but I do get excited during the chase.

HARRY: Tally-ho, huh?

LARRY: Yeah. It can be very exciting.

HARRY: I used to think of business that way, but…it's lost that appeal for me. It's just work now. *(Pause.)* I'm kind of glad our paths have crossed. I've been thinking I've needed a change, and—you know, I have friends—well, acquaintances, really—who are pretty avid bird watchers, and I have thought about trying it.

LARRY: You'd like it. You should give it a try.

HARRY: Yeah. It just feels like I'd be getting back to something real… essential.

LARRY: It is.

HARRY: But you know, if I did, I'd go out in the country. Nothing but pigeons and little sparrows in the city.

LARRY: Oh, no, no, no. New York is on a major flyway.

HARRY: I—what?

LARRY: I actually come in to the city this time of year because so many species come through Central Park during migration.

HARRY: More than out in the country?

LARRY: Well, depends on where you are, but, yes, you're guaranteed to see all kinds of species come through here. It's right on a major flyway.

HARRY: You said that. What's that mean?

LARRY: *(Enthusiastically.)* Every spring, this enormous river of birds comes up the Atlantic coast, and even though it splits, millions of birds continue right up the Hudson, over and through the city, many stopping in this park to feed and rest before they move on. That's why I come here.

HARRY: From the country.

LARRY: Well…not country…exactly…Long Island.

HARRY: Where—

LARRY: Have you seen <u>Winged</u> <u>Migration</u>?

HARRY: What's that?

LARRY: DVD. You can rent it. A beautiful film.

HARRY: And it explains how birds—

LARRY: Uh-uh, doesn't explain. That's the beauty of it. Just shows how birds move across the Earth. It's magic.

HARRY: *(Keys words into his Blackberry.)* OK. I'll get that. Sounds good.

LARRY: *(Stands and approaches the lake, holding the binoculars but staring out intently.)* Look at this-look at this-look at this. *(Lifts binoculars to his eyes.)* Yes!

HARRY: *(Stands from the bench and comes just behind LARRY.)* What?

LARRY: Here, you gotta see this. *(Points and begins to take off binocular strap without taking them from his eyes. Takes HARRY by the arm to pull him alongside himself so he can transfer the binoculars to him.)* See that duck?

HARRY: *(Peering out over the audience.)* That black bird on the water?

LARRY: Wait till you see him through these. Here— *(Moves the binoculars in front of HARRY'S face.)* It's a wood duck.

HARRY: *(Takes the binoculars to look.)* Uh...he's blurry.

LARRY: Use the knob. *(Places HARRY's finger on the knob.)*

HARRY: *(Leans forward at the moment of seeing.)* Wow. He's beautiful. He's gorgeous. He's not black—what color!

LARRY: That, my friend, is a find. If you, Harry, are starting your official bird list today, that's a hell of a start. A wood duck.

HARRY: *(Lowers the binoculars and looks at LARRY.)* I had no idea.

LARRY: Pretty cool, huh?

HARRY: *(Raises binoculars again to look.)* I thought you had to go to the tropics...or Africa to see that kind of color.

LARRY: That's what I was telling you.

HARRY: And these binoculars are great, bring me right in on top of him. And look at how far away he was.

LARRY: Yeah, a good set of binox are invaluable.

HARRY: *(Takes them down and holds them out to LARRY.)* Here.

LARRY: No, no, look a little more.

HARRY: No, he's gone, went around that point. Here.

LARRY: *(Takes the binox.)* Thanks. *(Looks out on the lake.)*

HARRY: *(Turns back to the bench and sits. Pause as he looks at LARRY from behind.)* Larry, why are you seeing a shrink—uh, a psychiatrist?

LARRY: *(Without taking binoculars down.)* Oh...I guess you could say... well... *(Lowers binoculars and comes back to the bench to sit.)* I guess you could call it... *(Pauses.)*

HARRY: It's OK, you don't have to tell me.

LARRY: No, you told me about...do I call it dishonesty?

HARRY: Yeah, sure—no, it's not so much dishonesty as just being... phony...not real. *(Thinks.)* Aaa, bullshit. Yeah, call it dishonesty.

LARRY: Well, you trusted me enough to tell me that, I should return the favor. *(Thinks.)* I guess you could say... *(Pauses.)*

HARRY: Skip it. It's OK. I was just curious because you seem like a pretty together young man.

LARRY: Thanks.

HARRY: I don't mean to pry.

LARRY: You're not prying. And I would like to tell you. It's just...

HARRY: Yeah. Forget it.

(Pause. LARRY fiddles with his binoculars, HARRY sits looking uncomfortable and starts to take out his Blackberry just as LARRY speaks.)

LARRY: *(Just before he speaks, begins to lift the binox to his eyes then puts them down and reaches into his coat pocket.)* Hey, look at what I have here. *(Pulls his field guide out of his pocket.)*

HARRY: *(Puts Blackberry back in his pocket.)* What's that?

LARRY: Roger Tory Peterson. His Field Guide to Eastern Birds. Best book on the market. I can show you a picture of that wood duck. *(Flips through the book.)* Here.

(Holds book up for HARRY.)

HARRY: Wow, this is almost better than the real thing.

LARRY: Ain't nothing better than the real thing, but the book allows you to verify that what you have seen is what you think you have seen. And there's all kinds of stuff about habitat, range, nesting, feeding habits.

HARRY: *(Leafing.)* And all these come here to Central Park?

LARRY: Well, not all, but—

HARRY: Look at these little yellow...they gold finches?

LARRY: Warblers, and they are a treat. Many of them come through the park here. But not for another couple of months. In May.

HARRY: Look at that one.

LARRY: A yellow. One of my favorites.

HARRY: Are those stripes really that red?

LARRY: Yup. But better than the book. The color of blood.

HARRY: *(Nodding his head solemnly.)* Wow. *(He hands the book back to LARRY.)*

Here.

LARRY: Thanks.

(HARRY stands from the bench and walks DS where he stares across the lake. LARRY watches his back but doesn't say anything. He puts his book back in his pocket.)

HARRY: *(Looks SR then at his watch then to LARRY.)* Well, I'm going to get out of here. It was real nice—

LARRY: *(Stands.)* Oh. Well. It was nice meeting you.

HARRY: *(Comes to LARRY and holds out his hand.)* You, too.

LARRY: *(Doesn't take his hand.)* Hey. I have a thought. How about we do some birding together? Meet here next Saturday and see what we can see?

HARRY: Yeah? *(Thinks.)* Yeah, I'd like that.

LARRY: Yeah, we should see some good stuff. Today is a little early for returning birds, but next week…should be good stuff. How about…eight?

HARRY: I'm up early. I could make seven.

LARRY: OK, seven then. Right here. *(Thinks.)* You'll have to get a pair of binoculars.

HARRY: Oh, right. Can you suggest a store—?

LARRY: No, wait. *(Hands his binox to HARRY.)* Take these and fool around with them this week. I have…god, I think I have seven pairs. I'll just bring one of those.

HARRY: Yeah? You'd give me yours?

LARRY: Not give. Lend.

HARRY: You'd lend me these?

LARRY: Sure. Wait. Tell you what. *(Turns and goes to the bench and picks up the hat.)* I'll take your hat for the week and give it back next Saturday.

HARRY: Naa, I don't want it. It's yours.

LARRY: You may change your mind. Anyway—*(Points at the binoculars.)*—you fool around with these this week and then you'll have a better sense of what to buy after you use them a bit.

HARRY: Don't you need them now? I mean, you're meeting up with your friend on the other side of the lake. Aren't you going to need them?

LARRY: No, we've been at it since eight o'clock. A look around this lake was the last thing on our schedule. It's OK.

HARRY: That's very generous of you.

LARRY: Not to worry. Oh, let me get your phone number. *(Takes out a pen and a scrap of paper.)* Just in case plans change.

HARRY: I'll give you my card. *(Goes into his wallet and extracts a business card.)* Has my cell and my email.

LARRY: *(Takes card then writes on the scrap. Holds the scrap out to HARRY.)* And this is my card.

HARRY: *(Chuckle.)* OK. *(Holds the binox up.)* So, thanks. Until next week.

LARRY: Until next week.

(They shake. HARRY peers SR for a moment then exits SL. LARRY watches him for several seconds then pulls off his knit hat and stuffs it in a pocket and places HARRY'S Russian fur hat on his head. He takes it off, looks at it then puts it on again, all the time facing SL.)

MARY: *(Enters from SR walking fast.)* God, I thought I'd never get out of there. So unlike Dr. Bernard. There was some kind of—*(Is just about to throw her arms around LARRY when she realizes he is not HARRY. Jumps back with a giggle.)* Oh, I'm sorry, I thought you were—*(LARRY turns toward her.)*

MARY: Lawrence. What are you doing here?

LARRY: *(Pause.)* Hi, Mom. I was wondering what was keeping you so long.
(Neither moves. Lights fall.)

(The End)

Standing from left: Sherry Zannoth *as GRAM,* Tamar Pelzig *as POO,*
Seated from left: Mike Connell *as MARCUS,* Julie Hays *as BETTIE*
and Alex Adams *as JUNIOR*
in TURKEY DAY by E. K. Deutsch

TURKEY DAY

By E. K. Deutsch

E. K. Deutsch is a multi-award-winning playwright/director, journalist, author, artist and composer and a member of the Dramatists Guild of America and BMI. Her plays have been produced regionally across the country, Off-Off Broadway and Off-Broadway. Her compositions for the theatre have taken her to the Finals in the BMI Lehman/Engel Musical Theatre Workshop, and her screenplay *Keeping Mum* brought her to the Semi-Finals in the American Accolades International Screenwriting Competition. Short plays have won Finalist and Top Ten Prizes at the LamiaINK! International Short Play Competition, and several of her full-length plays have been top winners in several playwriting competitions, including the TNT Playwriting Competition and The Little Theatre at Felician Playwriting Competition. Her one-acts have been performed for two straight seasons at the Barn Theatre New Playwrights Festival and at the Barebones Theatre Festival in North Carolina. Her play *Lost & Found* was nominated for 7 NJ Perry Awards, including Best Production of an Original Play, Best Direction, Best Actor and Best Actress and her play version of *Keeping Mum* was produced by the Arts Incubator Project at Kean University. She is a former member of the Shell Theatre Playwrights Platform at Times Square Arts Center in New York City, and a member of the Theatre Resources Unlimited Producer Mentorship Program in New York City. E. K. formed PIM Repertory group in 1998 to focus on the all-important discipline of script development, and development and production of new work for the stage continues to be her primary focus. With her partner Alex Adams, Deutsch is developing a "dramic strip", *Smart Alex Nation*, and continues to write and develop new work for the stage and screen.

Turkey Day made its New York City debut in April 2009 at The Shell Theatre Playwrights Platform. It was in the Final Four in The Riant Theatre's Summer 2009 Strawberry One-Act Festival at The Theatre at St. Clement's with the following cast, in order of appearance:

GRAM	Sherry Zannoth
BETTIE	Julie Hays
MARCUS	Mike Connell
JUNIOR	Alex Adams
LILA	Alison Crane
GRETA	Christina Calph
POO	Tamar Pelzig (Winner, Best Actress)

The play was directed by E. K. Deutsch (Nominee, Best Director)

CAST OF CHARACTERS

GRAM, a peppery family matriarch in her sixties.
BETTIE, a country housewife in her forties. Simple, cheerful, home-loving.
MARCUS, a farmer/welder in his forties. A salt of the earth family man.
JUNIOR, the youngest, late teens. Hostile, disturbed, overweight, explosive.
LILA, the oldest child, mid twenties. Lives to please others and keep the peace.
GRETA, a college student in her late teens to early twenties. Headstrong, outspoken.
POO, a young woman in her late teens to early twenties. Troubled, tortured.

SCENE I

(Thanksgiving. Present Day Arkansas. Early evening. The Dining Room of MARGARET SCHUMER and her recently deceased husband Henry, grand matriarch and grand patriarch of the Schumer family. A long table with a white tablecloth is set CS with eight chairs and a low centerpiece of large painted purple, green and orange pine cones and multi-colored spray-painted pine boughs. A doorway USR leads to an O.S. living room and a doorway USL leads to an O.S. kitchen. There is a hutch USR with glass cabinet doors in which the Schumer family china collection is displayed. MARGARET "GRAM" SCHUMER enters from the kitchen, her daughter-in-law BETTIE SCHUMER follows. Both women wear aprons, GRAM's is frilly and white and covers the front of her floral print

dress, BETTIE wears a full turquoise BBQ apron that says "KISS THE COOK" in large orange letters. Her apron covers her pink polyester pant suit. GRAM pauses USC and dabs her eyes with the white embroidered handkerchief she keeps in her apron pocket.)

GRAM: My first Thanksgiving without Henry.

BETTIE: I know Mamma P. It'll be all right. *(Brightens and changes the subject.)* Thank you for my new apron. I love it!

GRAM: *(Wryly)* Well, I thought it was you. *(GRAM crosses to a hutch SR and opens it.)* Let's use Mamma's set this year.

BETTIE: Eight-piece?

GRAM: Twelve once. Before the... *(Looks significantly at BETTIE)* accident.

BETTIE: Junior knows better now Mamma P.

GRAM: He take his meds? *(BETTIE nods, GRAM counts the plates inside the hutch.)* ...Seven, eight...nine serving plates, six...seven...eight bread plates.... eight... nine... ten... eleven.... twelve salad bowls. Thank the Lord.

BETTIE: Bowls don't work for skeet. *(GRAM nods)* Pretty pattern. Kinda pinky though. Thanksgiving's more green and orange.

GRAM: *(Irritated)* We'll use the cream colored.

BETTIE: Eight piece?

GRAM: *(Glares at BETTIE.)* Used to be.

BETTIE: *(Keeping the peace.)* Pink's fine. Goes with cranberry sauce. And salad. Pink and green. And butter and bread. I wanted to match the centerpiece. *(Gestures proudly to the centerpiece on the table.)* Junior made it in Special Ed.

GRAM: Never saw a purple pine cone before. Guess Junior has.

BETTIE: His art teacher says he's got imagination.

GRAM: So that's what they call it. If only you hadn't....

BETTIE: *(Interrupts in a patient sing song.)* It has nothing to do with those diet pills, mother, everyone says so, the doctors, everybody. Why don't you listen?

GRAM: *(Takes the plates out and hands them to BETTIE, who places them on the table.)* All I know is you didn't have to be in such an all fired hurry to lose your baby fat after Poo. *(Grumbles)* Five months along before you even noticed.

BETTIE: *(Smiles dreamily.)* He kicked.

GRAM: You can't tell me all that whoopee juice in your system didn't give Junior a wollop from the time he was a clump.

BETTIE: It was prescribed.

GRAM: You looked like a two by four with a gall in the middle.

BETTIE: *(Giggles)* Wondered why I couldn't get rid of that pooch.

GRAM: 300 pound pooch. 300 pound crazy as a bedbug pooch.

BETTIE: The meds. Put weight on him. He can't help it.

GRAM: Too bad it's a crime to eat your young.

BETTIE: *(Amused)* Junior'd make quite a meal. Which napkins? *(BETTIE opens a drawer on the hutch as GRAM arranges the plates on the table.)*

GRAM: The white, with the crochet.

BETTIE: *(Holds up a white napkin with lacy edging.)* I can't believe she sat there for hours making these.

GRAM: Mamma had concentration.

BETTIE: Mamma didn't have a life, says I. *(BETTIE crosses to the table with her hands full of napkins.)*

GRAM: Says you.

BETTIE: *(Pauses thoughtfully behind a chair.)* I wish I knew her before her brain went over.

GRAM: She woulda put the fear of God in Junior. He wouldn't need meds with Mamma around.

BETTIE: *(Giggles, sits and begins to fold napkin "birds" and place them triumphantly at each place setting.)* I laugh every time I look at that watch she left me.

GRAM: *(Stops what she's doing and chuckles.)* I'll never forget that morning. I wake Mamma and there she is, lying there with that watch strapped to her ankle. I say "Mamma, your watch is on your ankle" and she says to me, serious as can be...

BETTIE & GRAM: "Musta slipped down overnight!" *(Both women laugh companionably.)*

GRAM: *(Wipes her eyes.)* Thought I'd split a side.

BETTIE: She scared Poo something awful with that saw.

GRAM: Didn't like the look of her rocker, sawed it off.

BETTIE: Poo kept saying to me, "Mamma, do you think Great Gramma Mema likes my looks?" Poor child had Chain Saw Grannie nightmares for years.

GRAM: Mamma got real taken up with anything that stuck out. Had to take the saw away from her after a while, Henry thought sure she'd turn him into a capon when he wasn't looking.

BETTIE: *(slyly)* Wouldn't want that now, would we?

GRAM: *(defensively)* No.

(Loud male yelling O.S. from USR. BETTIE's husband MARCUS SCHUMER enters from USR holding a can of beer, followed by his son JUNIOR, a large, loud teenaged boy holding a giant bowl of potato chips. As he talks and stands he continuously stuffs potato chips in his mouth.)

MARCUS: Half time! (*MARCUS takes a swig of beer and wipes his mouth.*)

JUNIOR: Go Eagles!

MARCUS: (*Looks at the table with disappointment.*) You're no farther along? We gotta be done by end of half time!

GRAM: And what happens if we're not? Sun gonna fall from the sky?

MARCUS: A man deprived of his football? Too, too horrible Mamma. Too horrible for words.

GRAM: You can always abandon your family at Thanksgiving and take it in on TV trays. The turkey and the Eagles should get along just fine.

JUNIOR: When's dinner? I'm starved.

GRAM: This child ever stop eating?

BETTIE: He's growing, Mamma P.

MARCUS: (*Hugs JUNIOR as JUNIOR continues eating.*) He's my little linebacker, aren't you Junior? (*JUNIOR nods as he keeps eating.*)

GRAM: (*Pushes the men out of the room.*) We can't get anything done with you two lurking in here, go back and watch whatever it is they do at half time and we'll call you. Go! (*MARCUS and JUNIOR exit USR, GRAM grumbles as she and BETTIE continue to set the table.*) Like slopping hogs. I don't know why we bother with plates. Might as well stick everything in the middle and let 'em go at it with their hands.

BETTIE: I try Mamma P, but some things are wired in. They eat like they're late for a fire except Poo.

GRAM: Be 3 a.m. before Poo's finished. Never seen anything like it. One pea at a time. Don't know why you let her read at the table.

BETTIE: Keeps her calm, Mamma.

GRAM: She take her meds? (*BETTIE nods.*) Back in school yet? (*BETTIE shakes her head.*) Now how's she supposed to get herself a beau and make friends if she can't go to school? Seems to me those meds aren't doing a lick of good.

BETTIE: She doesn't have those awful attacks so much. We got her here, didn't we?

GRAM: Get new safety glass in the Chevy? (*BETTIE nods.*) That was a sight, Poo yowling and scratching at that glass like a rabid cat.

BETTIE: Something sets her off in the car. Especially when we're coming here.

GRAM: Maybe 'cause here's the only place you ever take her.

BETTIE: She's not bad when she goes to the doctor.

GRAM: Child's scared of her own shadow.

BETTIE: Not when she was little. Poo wasn't afraid of man nor beast. Something happened to set her off. She's gotten harder and harder to get through to Mamma. *(Sotto voce, confidential.)* We might have to put her into Brookhaven.

GRAM: That what her doctor says? *(BETTIE shrugs her shoulders.)*

BETTIE: Maybe.

GRAM: Poo in the loony bin. Junior could go along as a bodyguard.

BETTIE: I don't want to think about any of it today Mamma P.

GRAM: *(GRAM crosses to the USR doorway and yells O.S.)* Lila! Come down help us out! *(To BETTIE)* Thank the Lord for Lila.

BETTIE: She's my good girl. *(JUNIOR enters and crosses to the USL door. GRAM grabs his arm.)*

GRAM: Where you goin'?

JUNIOR: *(Defensively)* Need a little snack.

BETTIE: *(Indulgently)* No honey, you don't. We're going to eat soon.

JUNIOR: *(Whines)* I'm hungry! Just a little snack! I want a little snack! *(JUNIOR's voice rises to a high shriek and he begins to panic and shake his arms up and down rapidly. BETTIE crosses to him, holds his arms against him and speaks soothingly.)*

BETTIE: All right honey, all right. Go get a hot dog out of the fridge. *(JUNIOR relaxes, shudders a bit from his recent trauma and exits USL.)*

GRAM: *(Angry, to BETTIE.)* Spoiled. Spoiled rotten. Sixteen years old and still throwing tantrums.

BETTIE: You want him breaking plates?

GRAM: Can't control him, best take him where they can. *(JUNIOR enters happily from USL holding a fistful of cold, uncooked hot dogs. One hot dog hangs from his mouth.)*

BETTIE: That'll have to hold you 'til dinner honey. *(JUNIOR nods and mumbles unintelligibly with his mouth full as he exits USR. GRAM watches him exit with disgust.)*

GRAM: Never in my life seen a child eat cold hot dogs.

BETTIE: The package says "fully cooked" Mamma P. It's all right.

GRAM: Disgusting is what it is.

BETTIE: Better than butter.

GRAM: Thought I'd lose my breakfast first time I saw Junior eat a whole stick of butter.

BETTIE: Doing the best I can, Mamma.

GRAM: *(Darkly)* When's Greta comin'?

BETTIE: *(Looks at her watch.)* Bus came in at five. Any time now. Thanks for putting her up.

GRAM: Best keep the fox from the hen house. *(LILA SCHUMER enters. She is a demurely dressed, perennially sunny girl in her early 20's, eager and anxious to please.)*

LILA: What can I do, Grannie-pie? *(LILA hugs GRAM and kisses her cheek. GRAM smiles indulgently.)*

GRAM: Well, little darlin', go get the gravy boat, butter dish, creamer and sugar bowl and take 'em in the kitchen.

LILA: *(Crosses to the hutch.)* You want I should fill 'em for you?

GRAM: All except the gravy honey. Your Mamma's still workin' on that. *(LILA holds up the gravy boat.)*

LILA: The gravy boat. It's cracked. *(GRAM crosses to LILA and takes the gravy boat from her.)*

GRAM: Can't keep anything nice around here.

LILA: It's not bad. Like a hairline fracture.

BETTIE: *(Distracted, as she sets the table.)* It's old Mamma P. It's crumbling. Like Venice.

GRAM: Somebody knocked it around.

LILA: It'll be fine Gram. I'll put a little Crazy Glue on it to hold it tight. *(LILA exits USL.)*

GRAM: *(Grumbles)* Figures this family'd use Crazy Glue. *(A doorbell sounds O.S., BETTIE crosses USR.)*

BETTIE: I'll get it. *(BETTIE exits USR, voices are heard O.S. GRAM stands still and listens, then begins to bustle around the table, arranging plates nervously. BETTIE enters, smiling.)* Look who's here! *(GRETA SCHUMER enters from USR. She is pierced in numerous places, dressed in hippie/punk garb and carries a backpack. She tries to smile and almost succeeds.)*

GRETA: *(Monotone)* Hi Gran. Happy Thanksgiving.

GRAM: Hey girl. Give your Gram a kiss. *(GRETA crosses to GRAM and gives her a light peck on her cheek, GRAM hugs GRETA self-consciously.)* You can take your bag on upstairs to the guest room.

GRETA: Where's Lila and Poo?

BETTIE: Poo's upstairs reading, Lila's... *(LILA enters and sees GRETA. The two smile at each other and hug.)*

LILA: I missed you.

GRETA: Me too.

LILA: Gran, can I stay over with Gret?

GRAM: *(Relaxes)* Sure you can, honey.

LILA: Oh good. We've got a lot to talk about, haven't we?

GRETA: *(Shrugs)* Sure. *(GRETA exits USR, LILA follows her, then stops.)*

LILA: Be right back?

GRAM: Not too long now.

LILA: *(Cheerfully exits USR.)* OK! *(GRAM looks after LILA.)*

GRAM: That girl'd roll around in manure and come up clean.

BETTIE: I guess. *(BETTIE becomes pensive.)* Gotta do gravy. *(BETTIE brightens.)* One lump or two? *(BETTIE exits into the kitchen. POO SCHUMER enters tentatively from USR. She is a shy, frightened girl in her late teens. She wears a shapeless cotton dress and thick glasses and carries a thick book.)*

GRAM: What is it honey?

POO: Where's Mamma?

GRAM: *(Gestures with her head toward the kitchen.)* Gravy.

POO: *(Stops in her tracks.)* Oh.

GRAM: Something you want, honey?

POO: Quiet place to read. Lila and Gret are talking up a storm upstairs.

GRAM: Might be asking too much for a quiet place on Thanksgiving.

POO: *(Uncomfortably)* I guess... *(POO stands stock still and looks worried and undecided.)* I guess....I'll go out on the porch.

GRAM: Shouldn't be too noisy out there, except when trucks go by.

POO: *(Dreamily)* Trucks are OK. Like music.

GRAM: *(Confused)* Musical trucks?

POO: *(Confidentially, with animation.)* If you sit and listen Gram, you can hear the music. The birds are the woodwind section, flutes and oboes and piccolos, people banging on their houses with hammers, or cars thumping over the creases in the road bed, they're the percussion, the drums, you know? Trucks are deep and loud, like tubas, or maybe bass fiddles. And people talking, they're the strings, some high, some low. *(POO thinks.)* Sometimes the strings bother me. Gret and Lila are like strings right now, high and tight and stringy. And the rhythm goes on and on inside my head, all the time, keeping time, one two three four one two three four. Four four time, sometimes a waltz...one two three one two three one two three one two three..... *(POO waltzes around the table.)*

BETTIE: *(O.S.)* Mamma! Where's your cheesecloth?

GRAM: *(Gently, to POO.)* Uh, that's real...imaginative honey. *(GRAM yells O.S. as she crosses to the kitchen door.)* Behind the wax paper, in the middle drawer.

BETTIE: *(O.S.)* My hands are all greasy.

GRAM: I'll get it. *(GRAM exits to the kitchen. POO stops waltzing and crosses furtively to the hutch. She opens a bottom cabinet door and extracts a practically full flask of whiskey, which she secrets under her dress. She exits quickly USR. JUNIOR enters from USR licking his fingers and heads for the kitchen. GRAM appears in the kitchen door, stands imperiously in front of JUNIOR and holds out her hand like a traffic cop.)* Don't even think about it. *(JUNIOR opens his mouth to speak, GRAM stops him.)* Not a word. Back it up fella. And don't come back until we call you. *(JUNIOR tries again to speak, GRAM halts him.)*

Uhuhuhuhuh. And don't call out for your Mamma or throw a hissy fit. Won't work on me. OUT! *(JUNIOR sends daggers at GRAM and exits. GRAM looks skyward and smiles.)* Thanks Mamma. I thought so too.

(BRIEF BLACKOUT)

SCENE II

(The Schumer Dining Room, 15 minutes later. JUNIOR sits at the table and stuffs rolls in his mouth from a large basket of rolls. GRAM and BETTIE enter from the kitchen, GRAM snatches the basket away and moves it to the other end of the table.)

GRAM: *(Yells O.S. USR.)* Marcus! Time! *(GRAM moves closer to the USR exit and yells again O.S.)* Greta! Dinner! *(GRAM crosses to the USL entrance and yells O.S.)* Lila! Go get Poo off the porch! *(As GRAM calls everyone to the table JUNIOR has slowly pulled the basket to him and reaches for a roll. GRAM slaps his hand and moves the basket away from JUNIOR again.)* Now you stop that! Leave some for the rest of us. You know, girls don't like fatties.

JUNIOR: Don't like girls.

GRAM: Maybe if they had gravy all over 'em you would. *(MARCUS enters from USL, looks quizzically at the table, then at GRAM.)*

MARCUS: So where is it?

GRAM: Hold your horses. Don't you want to carve?

MARCUS: *(MARCUS picks up the carving knife and fork at the head of the table and carves a phantom turkey.)* White or dark?

GRAM: It's coming. Bettie's finishing up the gravy. *(MARCUS groans.)*

MARCUS: Game'll be over first. You can bet on it. C'mon boy, let's go. *(JUNIOR stands, MARCUS heads for the USR door.)*

GRAM: Freeze! *(The two stop in their tracks.)* About face! *(The two turn around.)* Sit! Stay! *(JUNIOR and MARCUS sit obediently, MARCUS at the head of the table. LILA enters from the kitchen with a pitcher of water which she pours into each glass. GRAM crosses to the kitchen door.)* Lila, keep an eye on 'em. How's she doing with that gravy?

LILA: *(Cheerfully.)* Still kinda soupy.

MARCUS: There's gravy in a can, isn't there for God's sake? Every year the same old nonsense.

GRAM: And she'll keep doing it every year until she gets it right. Bettie may be a lot of things, but she's no quitter.

JUNIOR: *(Mumbles.)* She's no cook either.

GRAM: You look like you've been eating good. Don't speak ill of your Mamma. *(BETTIE enters apologetically.)* Well?

BETTIE: Good as it's gonna get.

GRAM: Come on, let's haul it out. *(BETTIE, GRAM and LILA exit to the kitchen. POO enters from the USR doorway and sidles somewhat unsteadily into the room, book in hand.)*

MARCUS: Sit down Pumpkin. Time for the show. *(POO sits next to MARCUS and opens her book. MARCUS gently puts his hand on the book.)* Not now honey. OK? *(POO swallows nervously, nods her head and closes the book.)* Let's get this hoo-ha over with. Remember, make a big fuss when she comes out with the bird.

JUNIOR: *(As he rocks forward and back, which is his habit when not eating or otherwise distracted.)* Why do we always have to do this?

MARCUS: Your Grannie likes her Hallmark moments, son. Gotta humor her, else there'll be hell to pay.

JUNIOR: Like what?

MARCUS: You wanna eat? Make a fuss or you'll be suckin' air. *(GRAM enters, smiling broadly as she carries a large turkey on a platter. MARCUS, JUNIOR and POO begin to cheer and clap.)*

GRAM: *(GRAM smiles broadly and sets the turkey in front of MARCUS as LILA and BETTIE bring in bowls and plates of food and set them down.)* Came out pretty good this year. Hope it's not dry.

MARCUS: *(Stands and begins to carve.)* Every year, "hope it's not dry". And every year it's just fine, Mamma, juicy and tender.

GRAM: Where's Greta?

LILA: I'll get her. *(LILA exits quickly USR.)*

GRAM: *(To MARCUS.)* You keep carving.

POO: Said she wasn't hungry. Said she ate on the bus.

GRAM: What a surprise.

BETTIE: Mamma.... *(LILA enters, dragging GRETA behind her. GRETA wears an IPod and headphones, which she reluctantly removes, stuffs in her pocket and sits down.)*

GRETA: *(Drones.)* Hope it's not dry. *(LILA slaps GRETA playfully.)*

LILA: *(Teases.)* What do you care, little Miss Vegetarian?

BETTIE: What?

LILA: Greta doesn't eat meat anymore.

GRETA: *(Smiles wickedly.)* Except for recreational purposes.

GRAM: All right. That's enough.

MARCUS: No tofu turkeys around here.

BETTIE: *(To GRETA.)* You look thin, honey. You getting enough to eat at school?

GRETA: They try to stuff us like hogs. They figure it'll keep us quiet if we're packed to the gills.

MARCUS: It's paid for, you should eat it.

GRETA: So I can be a fat old freshman pig? No thank you.

LILA: Glamorous Greta. That's what they called you in high school.

GRETA: *(Sardonically.)* Yeah. I'm real glamorous.

GRAM: You studying hard? You gotta keep your scholarship.

GRETA: I don't have to study hard Gram, I'm sleeping with the Dean of Students.

MARCUS: Now you stop that.

GRETA: Why? She doesn't seem to mind.

LILA: *(Tries to defuse the tension.)* She's kidding, Daddy.

MARCUS: I'm not so sure.

GRETA: Does it matter?

GRAM: *(Grimly)* Let's say grace now, Missy. Join hands. *(EVERYONE joins hands around the table. Once all hands are joined GRAM nods and intones.)* Dear Lord, we made it through another year, and here we are again, thanking you for your bounty and honoring the memory of Grampa Henry, may he rest in peace in your sweet loving arms. *(GRAM gestures to the eighth, empty chair. POO fidgets and hiccups, LILA stares at her plate and GRETA makes a loud raspberry. GRAM rises and points her finger at GRETA.)* Don't you dare! You be quiet during grace! *(GRETA stands, gives GRAM and the empty chair the finger and exits quickly from the room.)*

BETTIE: Greta!

MARCUS: Let her go, honey.

JUNIOR: Can I have Greta's roll?

GRAM: *(Throws her hands up in disgust.)* I give up. Amen. And thanks to Greta for spoiling another family meal.

BETTIE: She's young and fiery Mamma. She'll settle down one day.

GRAM: She'll put me in my grave before that happens. If I let her. Which I'm not about to do. One day you're gonna run out of excuses for 'em Bettie, and then what?

LILA: *(With false brightness.)* That turkey sure smells good, Gram! And wait 'til you see the pies Gram and I made. Blue ribbon pies, I bet.

MARCUS: My Mamma makes the best pies in the county.

GRAM*: (Balance restored.)* Pass me some of that lump juice, uh, gravy, will you Poo? *(POO has disappeared into her book and doesn't hear GRAM)* She's gone. Son? *(MARCUS passes the gravy. GRAM, MARCUS, BETTIE and JUNIOR ad lib as lights go down.)*

(BLACKOUT)

SCENE III

(That night, late evening. The dining room. The table has been cleared of all but the centerpiece. Lights are low. Offstage sound of a door closing loudly. POO enters from USR. She wears a flannel nightgown and red sneakers. She carries the almost empty whiskey flask and walks unsteadily. She turns on the light switch by the archway leading to the living room, then crosses to the hutch to replace the flask in a bottom door of the cabinet. POO sways and dances around the room, pauses at Grampa Henry's chair, lifts her nightgown and shimmies out of her underpants. She pretends to dust the table with her underwear, then places it on her head like a bonnet and continues to dance with abandon around the room. GRAM enters from USR holding a rifle, which she sets against the hutch when she sees POO. GRAM wears a long-sleeved, worn cotton nightgown and soft slippers.)

GRAM: Poo! *(POO sees GRAM and laughs wildly as she continues her dance.)* What are you doing? I could have shot you. I thought you were a burglar, or a rapist.

POO: *(Giggles.)* Too bad for Greta I'm not a rapist. *(GRAM crosses to POO and waves her hand in front of POO's face as POO keeps dancing. POO sings.)* Grannie get your gun, get your gun get your gun. Take it on the run on the run on the run. *(GRAM continues to move her hand in front of POO's face.)* I'm awake Gram! I'm so awake! Do you hear it?

GRAM: Hear what? Stop now, Poo, you're scarin' your Gram. Now how'd you get here?

POO: I walked. No, I danced. Just like the red shoes. See? *(POO indicates the red sneakers on her feet.)* It's not so far, especially when you dance. Listen to the music, Gram, one two three one two three... *(POO hums a Strauss waltz and keeps dancing. The phone rings in the kitchen, GRAM crosses and exits to answer it. She is heard O.S.)*

GRAM: *(O.S.)* Yes, she's here. You better come quick. Bring her meds, maybe call the doctor. *(GRETA and LILA enter. LILA wears a demure nightgown and has rollers in her hair, GRETA wears bikini underwear and a skimpy undershirt. POO sees them and laughs loudly.)*

POO: You see? I got my own pajama party! Me myself and I! So there! Don't have to listen to the two of you... *(In a high pitched taunt.)* Yakyakyakyakyak like a bunch of chickens.

LILA: She's bad, Gran. What do we do?

GRAM: Your Mamma's coming.

LILA: She can't handle her. Sometimes Daddy can. Maybe you ought to call him. He's on night shift at the plant. *(GRAM crosses to the kitchen door and exits. GRETA crosses to POO and tries to restrain her, POO fights back with great strength.)*

POO: No, no, not this time! You can't always have it your way! You can't stop me. No one can stop me anymore. *(POO crosses to Grampa Henry's chair, picks it up and forcefully throws it DSR. LILA retrieves it and sets it next to the hutch.)* Not even you Grampa! Especially not you! *(POO holds her hands over her ears.)* Too loud! Stop! Too loud! *(LILA and GRETA maneuver POO into the chair and restrain her as she fights against them periodically in between flights of fancy.)*

LILA: What do we do?

GRETA: She smells like whiskey. *(Loudly, to POO.)* What did you drink, POO?

POO: *(Sways dangerously.)* Nectar of the Gods...manna from Heaven... lalala...

GRETA: *(To LILA.)* She got hold of something.

LILA: The doctor says she can't mix her meds with alcohol.

GRETA: No shit. *(GRAM enters.)*

GRAM: Your Daddy's coming. *(BETTIE enters from USR, stares at POO and the assembled company and begins to cry. She wears a floral cotton pajama set and slippers.)*

BETTIE: Oh no. Honey... *(BETTIE crosses to POO, POO sees BETTIE crying, becomes angry, shakes off GRETA and LILA and faces her mother accusingly.)*

POO: Why do you have to be so stupid, Mamma? *(BETTIE cries harder.)*

BETTIE: Oh Poo.... *(BETTIE pleadingly holds out a medicine bottle to POO.)* ...Honey, please take this...

POO: You don't know anything. You don't understand anything. You're stupid, stupid stupid.... *(POO pushes her mother away continues to dance around the room as she talks during the scene. BETTIE pursues her, POO plays a taunting game of keep away and manages to wrest the bottle from BETTIE and throw it US, where BETTIE retrieves it.)*

BETTIE: Poo honey, please stop. Please come with Mamma.

POO: I'm not going anywhere, anymore. And you can't make me. No one can make me. No one's going to stick me in a cage and stuff me full of pills. I hear you and Daddy talk at night in your bed about the crazy hatch. I'm not going there. I'm staying right here, and I'm going to dance, like the Red Shoes, dance to my grave, and you can't stop me. *(MARCUS enters from USR and gazes sadly at POO, who dances tearfully and defiantly.)*

MARCUS: What's wrong with my little Princess? *(POO sees MARCUS and begins to sob.)*

POO: Daddy.... *(MARCUS crosses to POO, she pushes him away.)* I can't love you anymore. I can't.

MARCUS: Pumpkin, let Daddy hold you and make it all better.

POO: Not you. Not you!

(POO starts to hit MARCUS with her fists, MARCUS holds POO's arms and tries to restrain her. She stops, startles and looks at him intently.) You look like him. You do. You know you do? *(POO breaks away. GRETA and LILA hold each other, girding themselves.)*

GRETA: Don't Poo. Please don't.

POO: Why? Did I beat you to it? What were you waiting for? *(POO stands CS and yells.)* Glamorous Greta Schumer drops atom bomb! News at eleven!

GRAM: What are you talking about?

LILA: Nothing Gram, nothing.

GRAM: What is going on Marcus?

MARCUS: Mamma, I have no idea.

POO: Stupid. All of you. Blind and stupid. You know why? Cause you wanna be. Cause knowing will kill you. Like it's killing me.

MARCUS: Where's Doc Ambrose?

BETTIE: Out of town. Got his service. Said we'd have to call an ambulance if we can't talk her down.

MARCUS: *(To POO.)* You hear that honey? You don't calm down, you'll have to go to the hospital. You don't want that, do you?

POO: Since when do I ever get what I want? You know what I want? You really want to know what I want? *(POO pushes the centerpiece aside wildly, JUNIOR retrieves it, POO climbs on top of the table, begins a sensuous belly dance and taunts GRAM as BETTIE and MARCUS move protectively toward her and hold their arms out in case she were to fall.)* I'm Salome, Gramma, and I want Grampa's head on a platter! *(POO yells.)* Bring me the head of Henry the Pervert!

GRAM: The child's gone insane.

POO: You wish.

GRETA: Stop!

POO: No! *(POO taunts GRAM.)* You wanna know? You really wanna know? *(GRAM turns away, crosses to the kitchen doorway and faces into the kitchen.)* No, you don't wanna know. Because you already know, don't you?

BETTIE: Mamma P? What's she talking about?

POO: *(To GRAM.)* You saw it didn't you? You had a front row seat, but you didn't want to stay for the show. *(To MARCUS.)* But I never said a word. You know why Daddy? Because I knew you'd hate me if I did. You'd hate me for ruining it all for you. Your wonderful, perfect father.

MARCUS: Poo, honey....

BETTIE: *(Growing concern.)* Mamma P, What's she talking about?

POO: *(Points her finger at GRAM, then at GRETA, LILA, and finally JUNIOR.)* I accuse! I accuse you, and you and you...and you! *(JUNIOR crumples, sits in the chair next to the hutch and starts rocking forward and back as his mother and sisters go to him.)* You all knew it, and you never said a word. Never, ever. *(To GRAM.)* Want to know why I read at the table Gram? Because he loved putting me on the table. *(Choked.)* Splaying me out like a roast pig, sticking his head up my dress, slurping at me like a nasty old dog, sticking himself in me, turning me upside down and sideways like a Kewpie doll. Reading takes my mind off it, and the music, taking up space in my brain, pushing him out. *(POO slumps onto the table, a shocked BETTIE moves to her and tries to hold and comfort her.)* But he keeps coming back. *(POO buries her head in her mother's bosom, GRAM collapses on a chair. MARCUS crosses to her.)*

GRETA: You weren't the only one.

POO: *(Tearfully.)* You proud of that? I'm not. But I bet if it was her precious Lila she wouldn't have walked away, would you Gram?

LILA: Stop it!

MARCUS: *(Angrily.)* Now you two stop right this minute! I've never heard such a pack of nonsense in my life. Mamma, do you have any idea what they're talking about? About Daddy? *(GRAM's head is in her hands, she does not respond. MARCUS shakes her gently as if to rouse her.)* Mamma? He didn't do that, did he? Mamma? *(GRAM pushes MARCUS away and replies in a monotone.)*

GRAM: He was a man, wasn't he? They do their nasty business wherever they can.

BETTIE: *(Choked, accusatory.)* Not to one of their own!

POO: *(Realizes.)* You were glad it wasn't you. I'm so happy I could be there for you, Gram. So happy he could do his nasty business all over me.

MARCUS: *(Dazed, emotions rising.)* I'm dreaming. I'm dreaming. Somebody wake me up.

POO: *(POO surveys the scene and her father's distress and realizes the impact her statements have made. She moves to her father for comfort, he does not respond, but stares at her in disbelief. POO makes a decision, shudders and addresses her family tearfully.)* I'll wake you up. I'll wake all of you up. And I'll be free! *(POO darts to the hutch, grabs GRAM's shotgun and exits quickly USR. MARCUS and BETTIE yell and chase after her, followed by GRETA, LILA and JUNIOR. GRAM stays in her chair, in a daze. A loud shot fires O.S., followed by screams, GRAM startles out of her tortured reverie and stands. Lights out.)*

(BRIEF BLACKOUT)

EPILOGUE

(One week later. Afternoon. The dining room. The dining table has been moved far USC, and six chairs are set up CS in a semicircle. Radio announcement during BLACKOUT.)

RADIO ANNOUNCER: *(V.O.)* "The funeral for Margaret Schumer was held today in Foleyville. The mentally ill young woman shot herself in the head in front of her horrified family on Thanksgiving Eve. It seems she was upset at the prospect of being committed to a mental hospital. She leaves behind two sisters, a brother, mother, father and grandmother and the sadness and mourning of a tightly knit farm community. Margaret Mae Schumer, dead at seventeen." *(Lights up. GRAM sits in a center chair. MARCUS sits at her SL side, BETTIE is next to him, and JUNIOR sits and rocks slowly forward and backward on the SL end, next to BETTIE. GRETA sits on GRAM's SR side, GRETA is on the SR end. They are all dressed in black. Gram's chair has more space on either side than the others, she is already being distanced by her family.)*

GRAM: Thought they'd never leave.

BETTIE: *(Dully.)* Never seen so much food.

GRAM: We got good friends. *(BETTIE begins to cry and rests her head on MARCUS's shoulder.)*

BETTIE: Oh Poo. If only we...

GRAM: Doesn't matter. She was wired in Bettie, like you say. Some people are wired for misery.

MARCUS: Those things she said, about Daddy....if I'd known, I could have stopped him. She could have been all right....

GRETA: She was afraid. Afraid we'd all hate her for telling. Especially you, Daddy. She couldn't live with you hating her.

MARCUS: I could never hate her. My little pumpkin. Why didn't she know that? *(MARCUS breaks down, GRAM reaches for him, but he recoils from her and breaks down in BETTIE's arms.)*

GRAM: Something else would have set her off. She was too sensitive for this world.

GRETA: *(Stands, turns accusingly to GRAM.)* End of story, right? Nice and neat. Forget the rug is so lumpy you can't walk on it anymore, with you sweeping everything under it. *(GRAM stands and she and GRETA face off CS.)*

GRAM: Your life will be full of stories, girl. This is just one of 'em. Better learn to move on. Enjoy what there is to enjoy. Nothing you can do about it now.

GRETA: *(Head to head with GRAM.)* So we're supposed to conveniently forget you were married to a sick man? Forget that stayin' at Gramp and Gram's meant that any old time we'd be taken from our beds in the middle of the night...

GRAM: *(Interrupts angrily, grabs GRETA's shoulders and shakes her, then releases her. EVERYONE reacts.)* Look around you! Lots of sickness. We all do things we wish we hadn't, and some of us can't help ourselves. You can't help being ornery, Junior can't help eating everything in sight, Poo couldn't help being afraid of the world and everything in it. That's the way it is. Let the marks turn into scars. Ever feel a scar? Twice as strong as unmarked skin. I got plenty of scars of my own... *(GRAM chokes and hesitates.)* ...some from the same well as Poo. *(EVERYONE reacts, GRAM sets her shoulders grimly and continues.)* Trouble makes you strong....or it kills you. *(GRETA crosses angrily toward DSL, BETTIE grabs her and restrains her lovingly. GRETA collapses in BETTIE's arms and cries. BETTIE gently takes GRETA back to her seat, GRAM sits and watches them. As BETTIE speaks she kisses her girls, then moves to MARCUS and JUNIOR and kisses and hugs them. BETTIE is now assuming the mantle of new Matriarch, the power shift is palpable.)*

BETTIE: That's the way it is. But we love you. We love you all very much. And we love Poo. *(BETTIE sits in her chair and cries as she clings to JUNIOR, who is overcome.)*

GRAM: *(GRAM has had enough, it's time to try to restore order and her fading position in the family. She speaks with great conviction and force.)* That's it. Your Mamma's got the idea. We've got to accept ourselves and everyone else for what they are... *(EVERYONE hesitates, then speaks as if in a dream.)*

BETTIE: A stupid simple woman...

GRETA: A bitch...

LILA: A goody two shoes.

JUNIOR: A big fat pig.

MARCUS: A blind man.

GRAM: And the woman who started it all. *(GRAM wipes her eyes.)* Time for a prayer.

(EVERYONE joins hands, GRAM pauses, choked. As she speaks POO enters slowly and beatifically from USL, dressed in a beautiful, brightly colored dress. She stands behind GRAM, smiles at her family with great love and looks out and upward.) My gravy boat broke on Thanksgiving Lord, after it drained its last drop. Broke in the dishpan while I was washing it. It got tired of carrying its load, and so did Poo. But we can't put her back together again, we're trusting that to you and your infinite glory. We know deep in our hearts she's whole and happy and smiling in Heaven today, all her worries gone, all her troubles erased by your love and care. We thank you Lord. Amen. *(The family mumbles*

their Amens, GRAM sings "Amazing Grace." There is a rapt pause at the end of the song.)

JUNIOR: *(With a catch in his voice.)* I need a little snack. *(GRAM bristles, POO laughs to herself and watches the scene with tenderness.)*

GRAM: You most certainly do not.

JUNIOR: *(Whiny voice escalates.)* I do too! I'm hungry. Those people ate everything before I could get to it. I'm starved.

BETTIE: *(Gently.)* Go get a hot dog out of the fridge, honey.
(Lights begin to fade as the conversation continues into the growing darkness.)

GRAM: I will not sit here today and watch you stuff your face with cold, slimy hot dogs mister....

MARCUS: *(In a daze.)* He's a growing boy Mamma.....

GRAM: Only way he's growing is horizontal. He's gonna start rolling around like a beach ball pretty soon if someone doesn't put a stop to this....

GRETA: Horizontal... *(GRETA giggles. At the end of the fade there is a special that lights GRAM's face and POO behind her.)*

(BLACKOUT)

(The End)

PRESCRIPTIONS

By Ellen Orchid

Ellen Orchid is an MFA graduate from the Actors Studio Drama School at Pace University, a Working Finalist at the Actors Studio, and a member of the Dramatists Guild of America. Her other plays include "Dream Wedding!", "To Moscow, To Moscow", "The Engagement Present", and "Criminal Mischief". As an actress, she had a principal role on "The Sopranos" (episode #48) and has appeared on Broadway (one night in the ensemble of "The Music Man", as well "Tony 'n' Tina's Wedding" (Off-Bway). As a stand-up, she has performed on TV and in many clubs. Her website is www.EllenOrchid.com. She is also an MD, specializing in psychiatry. She dedicates this play to her beloved parents, Walter and Adelaide, and her children, Deborah and Mark.

Prescriptions made its New York City debut on August 14, 2009 at the Theater at St. Clements. It was a semi-finalist in The Riant Theatre's Summer 2009 Strawberry One-Act Festival with the following cast, in order of appearance:

DR. RENEE BAYLOR Thesa Loving
ANITA VITALE   Ashley Adelman

The play was directed by Jessica Zweiman.

CAST OF CHARACTERS
DR. RENEE BAYLOR, 55, a psychiatrist
ANITA VITALE, 25, her patient

(It is November, 2009. Brooklyn Heights, an upscale neighborhood in Brooklyn,

NY. The living room of Dr. Renee Baylor's brownstone home. It is tastefully furnished and meticulously organized. There's a couch, center-stage, with an antique quilt draped over the back of it. Other pieces of furniture include: end-tables on either side of the couch, a coffee table, a stiff back, armchair, a book-shelf with old books, framed family photos, photo albums, an assortment of vases, an array of bird ornaments, and an expensive chess set has a shelf of its own, a small table with two chairs is stage-right, an empty birdcage next to it. The entrance to the kitchen is upstage right, entrance to foyer/front door is upstage center, and the way to go upstairs is stage-left.

LIGHTS UP ON DR. BAYLOR sitting on the couch, clad in a nice bathrobe after a shower. She is writing in a legal pad as though she has a deadline to meet. A dreamy Sinatra song is heard coming from another room. A suitcase, her pocketbook, and a briefcase are next to the couch, a pile of papers and a loose-leaf notebook on the coffee table next to her mug of coffee. After a moment more of writing, she tosses down the legal-pad, rises and disappears into the adjoining room. The music is shut off. The sound of rain is (now) heard. Dr. Baylor returns to the living room with a towel she uses to gently wipe her wet hair with. She sits on the edge of the couch, her gaze fixed on the legal pad. After a moment, she picks it up, reads what is written, when the doorbell rings, urgently. Startled, Doctor Baylor checks her watch. It is 9 AM. She stands, waits for a moment. The doorbell rings again even more urgently. She stuffs the pad under a cushion of the couch, ties up her bathrobe, goes to the door. Enter ANITA VITALE wet from the rain, with a well-worn duffel bag.)

DR. BAYLOR: Anita…You're early…*(Anita pulls out a box of pastry from under her jean jacket.)*

ANITA: I bought your favorite Italian pastries!

DR. BAYLOR: *(Looks at her watch.)* Two hours early…

ANITA: *(Apologetically)* I was up all night.

DR. BAYLOR: Are you OK?

ANITA: *(Trying to cover)* Kind of…

DR. BAYLOR: Oh?

ANITA: *(Trying to cope)* Rachel again…

DR. BAYLOR: *(Comfortingly)* Come in, come in…*(Puts an arm around her, ushers her in.)*

ANITA: Thanks. It's raining like crazy. *(Looks around the room.)*

DR. BAYLOR*: (Takes her coat.)* So what happened? *(Hangs the coat up.)*

ANITA: Last night Rachel flipped out, cut herself, and…*(Breaks down.)*

DR. BAYLOR: *Oh no…(Hands Anita a tissue.)*

ANITA: They told us she's gonna make it…

DR. BAYLOR: Thank God!

ANITA: *(Tiredly, Anita drags her duffel bag into the room.)* But what a night it was, let me tell you...

DR. BAYLOR: I can imagine. Is that all your luggage?

ANITA: Woulda been more but I had some stuff ripped off.

DR. BAYLOR: When I think of you in that place...

ANITA: First one up and out this morning!

DR. BAYLOR: Good...You should've called first, but good...

ANITA: Rachel *needs* somebody like you...

DR. BAYLOR: *(Modestly)* Well...

ANITA: I don't think she'd be cutting herself if she had *you* as her doctor! *(Before Dr. Baylor can respond, Anita hugs her with genuine affection.)*

DR. BAYLOR: Oh. *(Awkwardly, she accepts Anita's hug. Gently, but professionally...)* She'll be okay, Anita; she has *you* as her friend...

ANITA: *(Releases Dr. Baylor)* Yeah. *(Smiles)* Thanks for sayin' that.

DR. BAYLOR: Well, you're...*(Stops, anguished)* Your shoes are wet, dripping on the rug...

ANITA: *(Looks down.)* Oh, sorry, sorry, sorry...! *(Goes to move.)*

DR. BAYLOR: No, don't move! *(She grabs a towel, puts it down at Anita's feet.)* Step on the towel; take off the shoes, please. *(Anita does as she is told.)* The rug's from Paris, a family heirloom, one of a kind.

ANITA: Aren't we all! Right, Dr. B.? *(Hands Dr. Baylor her wet shoes.)*

DR. BAYLOR: *(Takes the shoes.)* Yes. *(Immediately wraps them in the towel. Then exits to the kitchen. Anita, in her tight jeans and loose-fitting blouse, checks the room out. It is the most beautiful living room she has ever seen.)*

ANITA: Nice digs!

DR. BAYLOR: *(From off-stage)* I don't know what that means.

ANITA: "Digs." *(Beat)* "Crib." *(Beat)* NICE HOUSE!

DR. BAYLOR: *(Re-enters with a clean towel.)* On behalf of the house, the "digs", thank you. *(Hands Anita the towel.)* For your hair.

ANITA: *(Italian, for "thanks")* Grazie...*(Rubs her head with the towel. After a moment, she laughs nervously.)* This is so weird!

DR. BAYLOR: *(At the coffee table, looking through her notebook.)* What is?

ANITA: Never done this before. What if I mess up?

DR. BAYLOR: *(Looks at Anita.)* Mess up with what? Be specific.

ANITA: Right, right, uh, I dunno, say your plants die, your house burns down---

DR. BAYLOR: I have faith in you, Anita...

ANITA: *(Cuts her off.)* That makes *one* of us!

DR. BAYLOR: You *must remember to* give yourself some credit.

ANITA: I tried. *(Beat)* Mastercard said, "Give it back!"

DR. BAYLOR: *(Feigns amusement.)* Oh. That's a good one.

ANITA: *(Proudly)* I should be a stand-up comic. People say that to me...

DR. BAYLOR: *(Back to the notebook.)* You're a natural. Now, if we could just get on with...

ANITA: *(Cuts her off again impulsively.)* Can I try this joke out on you?

DR. BAYLOR: *(Sits on the couch.)* I'd prefer to get down to business, okay? *(She picks up a journal-like book, flips through it, there are "post-it's" seen on every page).*

ANITA: *(Nervously)* Whoa, that's a lotta pages!

DR. BAYLOR: I'm just thorough.

ANITA: That make you a *thoroughbred,* Doctor?

DR. BAYLOR: *(Looks up.)* A "thoroughbred" is a...

ANITA: I know, I know, my dad was into OTB, so I know.

DR. BAYLOR: You mean "OCD". "Obsessive Compulsive Disorder."

ANITA: No. "OTB". "Off-track bettin'."

DR. BAYLOR: Oh. *(Silence.)*

ANITA: So where is it you're going again?

DR. BAYLOR: *(Doesn't look up, still reviewing her notes.)* A hotel in Manhattan.

ANITA: Cool. *(Beat)* What's the thing called that you're...?

DR. BAYLOR: *(Cuts her off.)* It's a psychiatric conference...a review course. Updates on the newest medications...for panic attacks...

ANITA: *(Nods, in response to the checklist of psychiatric disorders.)* Got 'em.

DR. BAYLOR: *(Continuing her list.)* ...Bipolar disorder...

ANITA: Got it...

DR. BAYLOR: ...Phobias...

ANITA: A few...

DR. BAYLOR: Attention deficit disorder...

ANITA: Check. *(Beat)* Hey! Throw in "fear of forgiveness" and you got my whole family!

DR. BAYLOR: Come on, you've been working very hard to stop identifying with...

ANITA: *(Cuts her off.)* I know, I know. *(Pause. Anita is restless like a little kid.)* I could never do what you do.

DR. BAYLOR: *(A beat. Sincerely.)* I bet you could.

ANITA: Thanks. *(A beat. Impulsively).* Hey. At the conference? Maybe I could "work the lounge" at your hotel, ya know? Show your fellow shrinks what I been like since you been helping me. Tell a coupla jokes, loosen them up... Get you some brownie points!

DR. BAYLOR: I don't think…

ANITA: What hotel is it?

DR. BAYLOR: Didn't I already tell you that?

ANITA: You said, "A hotel in Manhattan."

DR. BAYLOR: Oh. It's on the West Side. I'll get you the name when I get to that note. OK? *(Anita nods.)* In the meantime… *(She picks up the legal pad, businesslike.)* Here's the list of chores, listed as to their importance. For example—

ANITA: "Anita gets a cup of coffee," put as number one on the list.

DR. BAYLOR: *(Hesitates for a beat.)* All right. *(Rises, goes toward the kitchen.)*

ANITA: Thanks. I get a little spacey when I don't have my cor-fee, or, should I say, *more* spacey.

DR. BAYLOR*: (From the kitchen.)* It's very common, you should have told me.

ANITA: You're the best!

DR. BAYLOR: *(From the kitchen.)* You're helping me too, you know.

ANITA: *(Boasting.)* Today is eleven months and seventeen days, clean and sober. *And* away from Jake the Snake!

DR. BAYLOR*: (From the kitchen.)* Congratulations!

ANITA: If it wasn't for you, I'd be like Rachel, chained to a bed…or…

DR. BAYLOR: *(Pops her head out from the kitchen.)* You've worked very hard, Anita, don't forget that--- *(Returns to kitchen.)*

ANITA: You're the only one I can talk to.

DR. BAYLOR*: (Comes out of the kitchen with a fancy tray with nice cups and a pot of coffee on it.)* You'll make more friends soon.

ANITA: *(Beat)* I saw my mom yesterday.

DR. BAYLOR: *(Surprised)* Anita, what a big step for you!

ANITA: I went to see her at church. *(Beat)* "Our Lady of Perpetual Guilt."

DR. BAYLOR: *(Pours coffee into the cups.)* And did you speak to her?

ANITA: No.

DR. BAYLOR: No.

ANITA: *(Sadly)* Just stared at her back. She was in the first pew. I was in the last one… *(Drinks some coffee.)* She looked…small. And she wasn't wearing the scarf I gave her.

DR. BAYLOR: *(Puzzled)* You *expected* her to be wearing the scarf that you…

ANITA: *(Cuts in.)* I gave her this silk scarf, like, I dunno, four years ago for Christmas. Cost a ton, I swear. White silk with green ivy leaves. She loved it. She said it "was gonna be the only one I wear to church." And she always did.

DR. BAYLOR: Uh-huh.

ANITA: But…she wasn't wearing it.

DR. BAYLOR: Maybe it was being cleaned.

ANITA: Yeah sure, or maybe she threw it away, like she did with-

DR. BAYLOR: *(Cuts her off.)* Don't! *(Beat)* Now, going to the church was a big step for---

ANITA: *(Cuts her off.)* I want so much to have a new start with her!

DR. BAYLOR: You're getting that chance. Right here! *(Gestures around the room.)* Being here will build up your confidence, you'll see?

ANITA: *(Not totally convinced.)* Yeah, guess you're right. You usually are.

DR. BAYLOR: *(Looks at her watch.)* Uh-huh…Now…

ANITA: Are you close to *your* mom, Dr. B?

DR. BAYLOR: Um….

ANITA: *(Shrugs)* Just curious…

DR. BAYLOR: *(Stiffly)* I prefer not to answer…

ANITA: "…Personal questions," I know. But I thought because we're…

DR. BAYLOR: *(Stands)* I'm sorry, I didn't bring milk. How do you take your coffee?

ANITA: *(Joking)* I wait 'til the Starbucks guy's back is turned – then I take it.

DR. BAYLOR: Oh. I like that one. Whole milk or skim?

ANITA: Whole. *(Impulsively)* Unless you have "Half and Half"…

DR. BAYLOR: No. Sorry. *(Exits to kitchen.)*

ANITA: My mother always had "Half and Half". Now all I get from her is "Nothing and nothing."

DR. BAYLOR: *(Returns with milk.)* Let's look at those pastries.

ANITA: I hope she lets me home for Christmas. *(She picks up the box and uses her teeth to break the strings tying it.)*

DR. BAYLOR: Oh, please don't do that! *(She takes a pair of scissors from a drawer and gives them to her.)* You start with the pastry; I'm going to change out of this robe.

ANITA: *(Puts down the scissors.)* I'll wait 'til you get back. Don't like to eat alone. *(Puts milk in her coffee.)*

DR. BAYLOR: Neither do I. *(DR. BAYLOR leaves to go upstairs. ANITA picks up the "list of chores" pad. Looks at it, then rises from the table, the pad in one hand, her cup of coffee in the other. She slowly makes her way to the couch, fixed on reading the list of chores, when she trips, splashing coffee on a couch cushion. Panicking, ANITA puts down her cup and the pad, whispering.)* Shit,

shit, shit, shit, shit---! (*She uses her shirt sleeve to absorb some of the stain. Then quietly and quickly she dashes to the table for napkins. She runs back to the couch, wipes the cushion in furious strokes, stops to look at the stain but it's still bad. She lifts the cushion to turn upside down – in doing so she finds the pad/letter that DR. BAYLOR had tucked under the cushion at the top of the show. She throws it down, and works at getting the couch to look as it did before the accident. Suddenly, she remembers the pad she found, picks it up and before placing it back under the cushion, some writing on the pad catches her eye. She reads. After a few moments, she looks up from the pad, an expression of disbelief on her face. She tears out the front page, folds it up and stuffs it into her pocket, then returns the pad to where she found it. DR. BAYLOR is heard returning. ANITA grabs her coffee cup, scurries back to the table, and sits. DR. BAYLOR enters dressed in a nice suit. Anita turns to look at her.*)

ANITA: Looking beau-di-ful, Dr. B!

DR. BAYLOR: Thank you, Anita.

ANITA: (*Opening the pastry box.*) From Cuccio's, on Avenue X, home of the Vitale family and the best cannolis in Brooklyn.

DR. BAYLOR: They look delicious.

ANITA: Because they are. (*Beat*) *You* serve.

DR. BAYLOR: All right. (*She places a cannoli on a small plate and passes it to Anita with a fork and napkin.*)

ANITA: Grazie.

DR. BAYLOR: (*Serving herself.*) You're welcome.

ANITA: (*Eating*) You're super-important to me, Dr. B...

DR. BAYLOR: (*Smiles*) Careful with the crumbs.

ANITA: (*Suddenly*) This is so weird!

DR. BAYLOR: (*Startled*) What's the matter?

ANITA: Just drinkin' your coffee and bein' in your house IS SO FREAKIN' WEIRD!

DR. BAYLOR: Be more specific, please...

ANITA: (*Stands, panicking.*) House-sittin' for my shrink is so freakin'...

DR. BAYLOR: (*Cuts her off.*) Anita, come back to the table and sit with me. I told you, I don't like eating alone. Please, sit with me.

ANITA: (*After a moment, she returns to sit at the table.*) Have any of your other patients done this?

DR. BAYLOR: You're the first.

ANITA: That's me. "Top of the class!" High-five--- (*Anita holds up her hand to Dr. B who awkwardly obliges the return slap. They resume eating.*)

DR. BAYLOR: (*Finally*) Anita, promise you'll work at enjoying the comforts here, and ...(*Stops. Dr. B is visibly annoyed with Anita's messy way of eating. Anita is visibly nervous being watched. Rain is heard in the distance.*)

ANITA: *(Mouth full)* Hell of a day, right? Me coming early. Rain…

DR. BAYLOR: Right. Use a fork, please. *(Beat)* And eat over the table. Thank you. *(Beat)* The napkin is placed on the lap. *(Beat)* For the crumbs.

ANITA: This is the first time anybody ate a cannoli in this house?

DR. BAYLOR: Um, yes, I believe that's true.

ANITA: Another first! *(Holds up her hand for the Dr. to slap her "five" but it has cream on it. Dr. Baylor stares at it.)*

DR. BAYLOR: *I'll take a rain check on the slap-five thing.*

ANITA: I'm goin' to hold you to it.

DR. BAYLOR: All right. *(Looks at the list of chores.)*

ANITA: Bad luck not to return "the five," you know what I'm sayin'?

DR. BAYLOR: *(Doesn't look up.)* I don't believe in superstitions.

ANITA: I don't believe in "rain checks."

DR. BAYLOR: *(Looks at Anita.)* Is it the pastry bringing out this persistent behavior?

ANITA: *(Recoils)* Sorry.

DR. BAYLOR: Now take a look at the list and let me know if you have questions about anything.

ANITA: *(Takes the pad, looks at it.)* Uh…your handwriting is very good…

DR. BAYLOR: Anita, please. Any questions?

ANITA: How did you get it to be so…perfect-looking?

DR. BAYLOR: My mother was a teacher; now let's go through the list together. *(Takes the pad from Anita.)* Are you clear about how to lock the backdoor?

ANITA: I'm not clear about a whole bunch a things, Dr. B.

DR. BAYLOR: …which reminds me…your prescriptions. *(She goes to her purse, gets the prescriptions she wrote for Anita.)* OK. Your Adderalll. Your Depakote. And just in case you have a sleepless night…I prescribed something mild. Benadryl, if you need it. *(She holds out the prescriptions.)*

ANITA: *(Takes them.)* OK. *(Looks at them. A beat. Sharply, impulsively.)* There's this vending machine at the shelter. It's broken, you know?

DR. BAYLOR: *(Puzzled)* Could we just…

ANITA: *(Cuts in.)* Wait! So when you put the money in, the chips and things would move to the edge but they don't drop down. People would shake the machine to make the stuff fall down…

DR. BAYLOR: Anita…

ANITA: *(Anxiously)* Wait a sec, this is really cool…So, Sheba – she's the girl at the desk - she's my friend, right, so she gave me the key to the machine to get peoples' snacks out for them.

DR. BAYLOR: That's nice, but why are…?

ANITA: They call me "The Machine Girl." And when this guy, Luke, came in to fill up the machine, me and him had this little routine. He'd say, "Hey, Anita, when you getting' outta this dump?" And I'd say, "Why? You got a bed for me?" And he'd say, 'Yeah, but my wife's usin' it!" Hey! *(Stands)* I forgot to give the key back! They won't be able to get their stuff! *(She reaches for the key which is on a string around her neck and shows it to Dr. B.)* Where's my coat? Can you get it for me?

DR. BAYLOR: *(Reassuringly)* I'll take care of the key situation on my way to the conference.

ANITA: Oh?

DR. BAYLOR: I don't want you going back to that place for any reason. *(She gently removes the key from around Anita's neck.)* Anita, promise me you won't invite anyone over here. *(Anita nods.)* There are valuable antiques my parents spent a lifetime collecting.

ANITA: WHERE ARE YOUR PARENTS? *(Beat)* Florida?

DR. BAYLOR: *(Moves back to the table where the coffee and pastry is set.)* No. They're deceased.

ANITA: Oh. Sorry.

DR. BAYLOR: They were old. *(Starting to clean up.)*

ANITA: *(Softly)* Why do people say "deceased"? Why isn't it just "ceased?"

DR. BAYLOR: *(Beat)* Everything stops, either way. *(Pause. Rain heard.)*

ANITA: *(Anita takes a breath. Walks to the table to join Dr. B.)* Tell me what you want me to do.

DR. BAYLOR: *(Grabs the legal pad, talks fast.)* OK. The usual chores: dishes, re-cycling, vacuuming, dusting, sweeping, water the plants – there are post-it's on each plant with its watering schedule. Um,get the mail and leave it on the lacquer table.

ANITA: The what?

DR. BAYLOR: The Chinese table by the front door. Please remember to remove your shoes when you come in. In the kitchen, third-drawer left of the stove, there's an envelope with cash, and… *(Stops. Looks at Anita who is fiddling with the birdcage on a table.)*

ANITA: What's with the birdcage? Did you bird die?

DR. BAYLOR: Birds. "Zac and Zoe". Pretty little singing birds.

ANITA: "Zac and Zoe" sound like cartoon bird names.

DR. BAYLOR: Short for "Prozac" and "Zoloft." My father named them.

ANITA: When did they die?

DR. BAYLOR: Who?

ANITA: The birds.

DR. BAYLOR: They didn't die. I let them go. *(She continues to clean up)*.

ANITA: *(Smiles nervously.)* Didn't think I could handle them?

DR. BAYLOR: Oh, no. No. They'd been caged long enough.

ANITA: Do you know what happened to them?

DR. BAYLOR: No. Once, I thought I heard them, but now I'm certain it was just my mind playing back a time when they *were* here.

ANITA: Were they kinda like your kids?

DR. BAYLOR: I suppose.

ANITA: Were you ever married?

DR. BAYLOR: No.

ANITA: So there was never a "Mister B?"

DR. BAYLOR: My father was "Mister..." (Corrects herself) "Doctor B."

ANITA: Was he a shrink too?

DR. BAYLOR: Chief Psychaitrist at "Long Island Medical". *(She continues to organize her papers.)*

ANITA: He must've been so proud of...

DR. BAYLOR: *(Cuts her off, looks up.)* And if I *had* a husband, his name wouldn't be "Mister B.", would it?

ANITA: No.

DR. BAYLOR: It just didn't happen for me.

ANITA: OK.

DR. BAYLOR: Actually, it's not that "it didn't happen for me." I didn't *want* it. I never *met* anyone I *wanted* to marry.

ANITA: *(Watches Dr. B tie up the pastry box and pile up plates, etc.)* So---where do I sleep?

DR. BAYLOR: My room. Up the stairs – first door on the left.

ANITA: In your bed?

DR. BAYLOR: *(Stops. Looks at Anita)* Yes.

ANITA: I can just sleep on the couch.

DR. BAYLOR: Why would you choose to sleep on the couch when---

ANITA: *(Cuts her off)* I dunno, it's just kinda weird to sleep in your therapist's bed...

DR. BAYLOR: It's a first-class posture-pedic mattress!

ANITA: I dunno, it's just...

DR. BAYLOR: *(Cuts in.)* Don't say "weird"! You're twenty-five years old, can't you come up with a better word than...

ANITA: It's psychological.

DR. BAYLOR: What?! *(Gives up.)* Sleep wherever you like.

ANITA: And it's just for one week, right?

DR. BAYLOR: Right. Just one week.

ANITA: *(Anita moves to help clean off the table.)* Then you're comin' back. One week from today.

DR. BAYLOR: *(Increasingly impatient.)* Yes! Now! Please. I'll clean. Why don't you...

ANAITA: I wanna help, Dr. B, no big...

DR. BAYLOR: *(Snaps)* I don't need your help, so go and...

ANITA: *(Spills the container of milk.)* Shit!

DR. BAYOR: *(Picks up her list of chores to keep it from getting wet.)* Move away from the table ---please!

ANITA: Sorry!

DR. BAYLOR: *(Furious, wiping the table.)* I told you to move away from the table...

ANITA: Lemme help I did it, so let...

DR. BAYLOR: *(Dr. B has a strong impulse to push Anita away from the table, resists doing this, tries not to touch her, instead using her tone to accomplish this.)* I'll do it! You complicate things! Have a seat! *(Anita stands frozen, afraid to move, fixed on Dr. B who is on her hands and knees wiping the carpet.)* I am so tired of cleaning up everybody's goddamn messes! Literally and figuratively... *(She stands up, glares at Anita.)* That table accident could have been avoided so easily with a little common sense. You have to stop acting so impulsively. Have we not gone over that a million times?!!!

ANITA: *(Kindly)* What's botherin' you, Dr. B?

DR. BAYLOR: *(Furious, indignant.)* What's "botherin'" YOU?

ANITA: I'm nervous about...

DR. BAYLOR: Why?? It's very simple. If you'd listen instead of interrupting and rambling on about vending machines and... *(Stops herself suddenly. Takes a moment to try and calm herself down.)* I...uh, I didn't sleep well last night so I'm a little short on, um, patience...Look, I'm sorry. And... *(Looks at her watch)*, I have to go.

ANITA: *(Suddenly)* I don't think there is a conference!

DR. BAYLOR: What?!

ANITA: *(Decisively)* Somethin' else is goin' on.

DR. BAYLOR: Excuse me? What else is going on? I have to go!

ANITA: I don't think you do! *(Pulls out the piece of pad paper from her pocket and unfolds it.)* Why did you write all this stuff about...

DR. BAYLOR: *(Realizes what Anita has, explodes.)* WHERE DID YOU GET THAT??! *(Reaches for it but Anita quickly moves away.)* HOW DARE YOU GO SNOOPING AROUND MY...!

ANITA: I found it 'cause I'm clumsy, not because I was...

DR. BAYLOR: *(Cuts her off.)* What?! *(Again, reaches for the paper but Anita is too quick and moves away.)*

ANITA: Why'd you write this stuff?

DR. BAYLOR: IT'S NONE OF YOUR BUSINESS!

ANITA: It *IS* my business! Canceling me outta your life – like I'm a subscription to a magazine – is *MAKIN'* it my fuckin' business!

DR. BAYLOR: *(Desperate)* This...this was a mistake...

ANITA: *(Waves the paper at the Dr.)* You're really gonna go and...

DR. BAYLOR: *(Cuts her off.)* Stay out of my life!

ANITA: "Stay out of your DEATH", you mean.

DR. BAYLOR: YOU"RE BEING RIDICULOUS!

ANITA: You made up the conference, you let your birds go, and thinkin' maybe I wouldn't notice, you wrote my scripts with six months of refills! You NEVER did that before!

DR. BAYLOR: *(Exasperated)* GET OUT OF MY HOUSE!

ANITA: *(Reads from the paper.)* "Dear Anita,"...

DR. BAYLOR: Oh no...Please don't...

ANITA: *(Continues)* "...I leave you all that I own. My life is in re-runs now. No new episodes. Or none that I want, anyway. I am doomed to pain, to pain, to pain..."

DR. BAYLOR: *(Shattered, despairing)* You don't understand...what I...

ANITA: *(Looks down at the paper.)* You wrote the same paragraph over and over...

DR. BAYLOR: *(Nods. Softly.)* Yes. Um... It was a little...uh...self-hypnosis that I was...And then you came early and...a... *(Overwhelmed with sadness.)* Anita, my parents killed themselves, a year ago today. I found them upstairs in their bed, arm in arm... *(Beat)* Overdose. They didn't say goodbye, didn't leave a note, and believe me ---I looked everywhere, but... nothing. My mother was a proud and independent woman, a perfectionist, an intellectual...She suffered greatly due to a stroke. With her mind affected, she got so angry, always annoyed *and* annoying, she couldn't reach up to turn on the lights anymore. Dad, arthritic and withdrawn, lived in the TV. *(Beat)* A man of superior qualities, he had reached the place of "having nothing more to say."

ANITA: I...I'm so sorry...

DR. BAYLOR: They were suffering, but it never occurred to me that they would take their lives... *(Beat)* They were my dearest friends. My only friends, really. And they left me. *(A beat)* We loved the same books, plays, music, always traveled together, and before their bodies began to break down, we *(manages a smile)* never argued. *(She is lost in thought for a moment. ANITA stares at her, unsure of what to do or say.)* The thought of going to see a therapist and being told I'm stuck in the "spoiled 'only child' syndrome" and that "It's time to grow up" which will "make me less afraid of getting closer to men." *(Beat)* I KNOW THAT! I KNOW ALL THAT! I KNOW ALL ABOUT ABANDONMENT ISSUES! I KNOW ALL ABOUT... *(She looks at Anita who has her hands in her pockets, visibly at a loss, and stops speaking.)*

ANITA: *(Finally)* It must've been bad... because you didn't think of what killin' yourself...would do to me...

DR. BAYLOR: *(After a pause, softly.)* I...I thought... if I left you all I owned...that you'd...

ANITA: ... What. Become a stronger person? Be healed? Your parents left *you* all *they* owned...

DR. BAYLOR: *(Nods. Manages a smile, impressed by ANITA'S insight.)* Anita...Come here... *(ANITA steps closer, waits a beat. DR. BAYLOR holds up her hand, the palm facing Anita. After a beat. ANITA "slaps" the Dr. "five". They share a smile. A beat.)* My head is throbbing. *(ANITA gently guides her from the dining table to the couch and helps her stretch out on the couch. She places a throw pillow gently under DR. BAYLOR'S head. She puts the quilt over her, sits by her, stroking her hair gently, to comfort her. Softly.)* Anita?

ANITA: I'm right here...

DR. BAYLOR: *(Exhausted)* I wrote your mother a long letter. *(Beat)* It's... going to be a nice Christmas this year. *(Beat)* Anita?

ANITA: *(Continuing to comfort her, stroking her hair gently.)* I'm right here. *(A beat. The sound of the light rain falling is replaced by the song, "How Fragile We Are," as the lights do a slow fade to black.)*

(END OF PLAY)

Frank Winters (seated) *as ANDREW* and Steven Michael Laing *as DANIEL*
in FIREMAN by Stephen Brown

FIREMAN

By Stephen Brown

Stephen Brown recently received his undergraduate degree from Trinity University in San Antonio, TX before moving to New York. Since then his plays have been produced or developed at the Kennedy Center, American Globe Theatre, Theatre at St. Clements, Access Theatre, as well as in New Jersey, Texas, and California. He has won three grand jury prizes at various short play festivals around the country as well as a Mach Fellowship to develop the play *Sandbox*.

Fireman was a semi-finalist for the Source Festival in D.C. before making its New York City debut in July of 2010 in the Rapscallion's Salute UR Shorts Festival at the Access Theatre. It was a semi-finalist in The Riant Theatre's Summer 2010 Strawberry One-Act Festival at the Theatre at St. Clements with the following cast, in order of appearance:

ANDREW   Frank Winters
DANIEL   Steven Michael Laing

The play was directed by Stephen Brown.

CAST OF CHARACTERS

ANDREW, a 20-something former fireman. His face has recently been disfigured and he wears a mask to hide it.
DANIEL, a 20-something graphic designer. Andrew's boyfriend.

SCENE I
(The stage is bare except for a kitchen table with two chairs. ANDREW, mid-twenties wearing pajamas that have obviously been worn for days and a mask on his face enters carrying an armful of grossly discolored paper towels, crosses the stage and exits. A radio turns on from offstage. Andrew re-enters carrying a bottle of aspirin and places it on the table along with a bowl and spoon. He then stops at the table, turned upstage, and slowly reaches up to feel his mask. He then barely takes off his mask, and equally as slowly feels his face underneath. His entire body posture slowly sinks to the ground, as if finally succumbing to gravity. Finally, he puts his mask back on and exits, returning with a bowl of frosted flakes, pouring them into the bowl and sitting down, quietly taking in the music.)
 DANIEL: *(Offstage)* Oh God, help me.
(DANIEL enters wearing black slacks, no shirt, and a robe. He's holding his head.)
 DANIEL: Aspirin. Mother of shit, aspirin.
(Daniel sees the aspirin on the table and does his best with a smile.)
 DANIEL: Good morning.
(He takes the bottle of Aspirin and looks at the cereal, pointing at it and back to him.)
 ANDREW: I don't eat Frosted Flakes.
 DANIEL: Love you.
(Daniel kisses Andrew on the head, then opens the Aspirin and pours many pills into the cereal.)
 DANIEL: Who are we listening—
 ANDREW: Don't talk. Eat. You're already going to be late.
 DANIEL: For what?
 ANDREW: Work.
 DANIEL: …it's Saturday.
 ANDREW: …it is?
 DANIEL: Yeah—
 ANDREW: Wait. Wednesday, the 23rd, / Thursday the 24th…
 DANIEL: Today is Saturday, the 29th. An official yogurt and weed day… holiday.
 ANDREW: It's Saturday?
(Daniel gets up and takes his cereal offstage.)
 DANIEL: If you saw the outside of this room every once in a while…
 ANDREW: Right. Where are you going?
 DANIEL: *(Off)* Needs milk…You know, you really should've come out last night.
 ANDREW: I was tired.
 DANIEL: *(Off)* You're conveniently tired a lot.

(Daniel re-enters with the cereal and jug of milk.)

DANIEL: And Friday used to be our night. Going out dateless just… feels like I'm back high school.

ANDREW: Doesn't stop you every other night of the week.

DANIEL: But Friday night's special…Paul and Gary asked about you. Again. They're starting to think we broke up.

(Beat.)

ANDREW: Good for Paul and Gary.

DANIEL: They introduced me to their "friend" last night, Garth—this fake-tan, bald guy who clearly shaves his entire body. The man literally looks like a human penis. Milk?

ANDREW: For what?

DANIEL: To drink.

ANDREW: No, thank you.

(Daniel chugs milk from the jug, easily spilling most of it down his chest.)

ANDREW: What time did you get in last night?

DANIEL: Two—three something, probably…It was dark.

ANDREW: It was 4:37.

DANIEL: Here's the bigger question, was that what time I walked in? Or what time I projectile-vomited all over my cheetah lamp? … thank you for cleaning that up, by the way.

ANDREW: What did you guys do?

DANIEL: Come out next time and you won't have to ask.

ANDREW: I don't remember staying out that late when we went out.

DANIEL: Yeah, we'd stay out till 4:34, 4:35, latest.

ANDREW: Was Garth a good dancer?

DANIEL: Not really. It was like dancing with a seizure victim on speed. He also tried to bring back the robot.

ANDREW: I see.

(Pause.)

DANIEL: *(Amused)* You're angry.

ANDREW: It was just a question.

DANIEL: "Just a question". A question about how the-human-penis-man Garth dances. Was the next question going to be whether or not I got a number or what his cock tasted like?

(No answer.)

DANIEL: You're serious.

ANDREW: Gary and Paul didn't have problems imagining the idea.

DANIEL: Gary and Paul voted for Bush. Twice. And nothing has changed. Nothing has or will change…you stupid…fucking idiot.

ANDREW: Thanks.

(Daniel kisses Andrew on the mouth, but the mask is in the way. Daniel attempts to lift it up, but Andrew stops him.)

DANIEL: Let me kiss you.

ANDREW: So kiss me.

DANIEL: Let me really kiss you…I don't care.

ANDREW: I care.

DANIEL: I also don't give a shit about what you think.

ANDREW: Yes you do.

DANIEL: We'll just take it off and pretend it never happened, okay? We won't even talk about—

ANDREW: Stop.

DANIEL: Just this once—just for a moment—

ANDREW: Stop!

DANIEL: It's barely noticeable, I won't—

ANDREW: What's sixty percent of your face?

DANIEL: Wha—what?

(Andrew puts his hands on Daniel's face and starts drawing an outline with his fingers.)

ANDREW: …your beautiful face. The cheek, the nose, your entire forehead and right eye, the tense part of your jaw and the brown and blonde stubble on your chin that arrives at 9 o'clock at night without fail. Above all the smoothness…the smoothness…and your lips. Sixty-three percent. There's nothing left to kiss.

(Pause.)

ANDREW: Eat your cereal.

(Daniel grabs Andrew's hands.)

ANDREW: What are you doing?

DANIEL: Dance with me.

ANDREW: *(Groans)*

DANIEL: Don't be a grump, dance with me. Make up for all those lousy lap-dances I had last night.

ANDREW: Jesus, your breath smells like vodka cranberries.

DANIEL: And it tastes like vomit.

ANDREW: Well, I'm glad you had fun.

(They dance.)

DANIEL: Go on a picnic with me today.

ANDREW: No.

DANIEL: Please?

ANDREW: Will you stop dancing?

DANIEL: Yes.

ANDREW: … Okay.

DANIEL: Okay?!

ANDREW: Sure.

DANIEL: Sure, okay…really? Where do you want to have it? You choose.

ANDREW: Since I know you want to relax, why don't we lay down a few blankets in the living room? We can—

DANIEL: Fuck the living room, the park—Harrison Park, by the beach. We'll bring your snoopy blanket and set up by the swings.

ANDREW: It's Saturday though, there are kids—

DANIEL: It's okay, I'll beat the shit out of them until they leave.

ANDREW: Dan! We—

DANIEL: I don't mean literally. But look, you, me, the snoopy blanket, lots of whipped cream, yogurt, and a little bit of weed? We could play on the playground like the immature adults we are, then when it gets dark, maybe streak down the beach and into the dark ocean like we used to…yeah?

ANDREW: Or, since it's freezing outside, we should lay down some blankets in the living room, buy some real food—and whipped cream. We could still streak around the living room, and this way we won't get arrested.

DANIEL: Or we could skip the park and go straight to the beach. Bury ourselves in the sand right next to each other. If it's as cold as you say, people won't even be out there. We could start our own neo-hippie revolution *(Daniel kisses him on the neck.)* Just you and me *(Kisses him on the neck again.).*

ANDREW: How about I just—stop. That tickles.

DANIEL: I know.

(Daniel continues kissing him.)

ANDREW: Why don't we just stay in and I'll make us some… *(distracted by kissing.)*…something…to eat—

(Andrew gives in and the two start kissing each other, possibly falling back on the table or knocking over a chair. Daniel attempts to take off Andrew's mask, but Andrew stops him.)

DANIEL: *(Whispering)* Take this off.

(Daniel attempts to take off his mask again. As Andrew stops him again, the two struggle over it, neither giving up, until Andrew backs away out of Daniel's grasp. They stand apart for a moment, out of breath, then Daniel goes towards Andrew.)

DANIEL: I didn't mean—

ANDREW: Don't touch me…why? Why do you do this? What is this obsession with refusing to listen? You have to—

DANIEL: Obsession / is it?

ANDREW: —You have to, don't you? You can't get enough of pissing me.

DANIEL: Well, if you're going to leave that thing on, could we at least get some removable parts for it? You know, sort of like Mr. Potatohead?

ANDREW: Jokes.

DANIEL: Seriously, I think it might go really well with a handlebar moustache or some groovy sideburns.

ANDREW: Careful dear…tread lightly.

DANIEL: I've been tip-toeing for a while now, *Sweetie*. I kept quiet when you removed all the mirrors and even joked when you stopped letting people come over—

ANDREW: —that was your idea!

DANIEL: —but I see you everyday with that thing on your face and—it looks fucking stupid! It's always looked fucking stupid! It was a stupid fucking idea from day one!

ANDREW: Fuck you!… You never had to look in the mirror, praying to see something different. You've never felt your face burn away! Actually felt fire attach itself to your skin and melt your fucking nose off while you tried to scoop your skin off the floor and put it back where it belongs. My face is a stain on the scorched carpet of that burnt out house…They could put me in a cage and display me at a freak show next to the bearded woman; 8th wonder of the world, the man who fought fire and lost. My face is pain incarnate, it never stops burning!… Does it still look fucking stupid now?

DANIEL: Yes.

ANDREW: You pretty, perfect, unflawed man, why don't you go fuck Mark the dancer, or have a 3-some with Gary and Paul, or do whatever the hell you do every night you go out—

DANIEL: I already did! I fucked 'em all Andrew, I fucked 'em all and I loved it. I'm the toast of the town, baby. When I go out, men get in single-file and I just go down the line; bean bags and mushrooms in each hand. Fuck, I could open up my own sperm bank if I didn't swallow so much. I've had so much sex I even fucked a woman by accident; I was just pumping it into any hole I could find…and it's all for you, sweetheart.

(Long pause.)

DANIEL: I haven't gotten laid in four months…since we last…I thought about cheating, but I…

(Daniel goes to Andrew.)

DANIEL: I know what's under there *(gesturing to Andrew's mask)*. Right here, two perfect brown eyes…one a little lazier than the other, and eye-lashes like the Snuffleupagus monster from Sesame Street. A nose that twists to the left because your brother's an asshole and threw the TV remote at you when you were kids. Three cute little freckles near your left ear, underscored by a perfect jaw. Your lips...*(sigh)* your lips...a tiny upper lip and a much larger lower one, as if it were trying to compensate for your upper lips inferiority complex... I see and feel every part of your smooth, imperfectly beautiful face. You're not a leper, and I would still love you even if you were one...unless your cock fell off, of course. Once that goes, I'm pretty much done with you and your bitching...but for now...you're pretty much all I want.

ANDREW: ... fag.

DANIEL: Hypocrite.

(Daniel kisses the lips of the mask, then brings his hands up to it. Andrew grabs a hold of Daniel's hands, but doesn't stop him. Daniel, very slowly, takes a hold of Andrew's mask and removes it from his face.)

DANIEL: There you are.

(Pause. Then Daniel takes Andrew's hand and slowly brings it up to his face, drawing the palms of their hands over it ever so gently and subtly.)

DANIEL: See? Smooth...ever so smooth...

(Blackout.)

(The End)

Colin Knight *as JEFFREY LEWIS* and Jason Faust *as STEVE GAILEY*
in HEROES by Joseph Lizardi

HEROES

By Joseph Lizardi

Joseph Lizardi is an ESL teacher at Clinton High School in the Bronx, a Member of the Dramatists Guild of America, Inc., and he has been a Playwright-In-Residence at many theatres, specially at the Arena Players Repertory Theater in Farmingdale, New York. His one-act and full-length plays have been produced Off-Off-Broadway, Off-Broadway, and at Regional Theatres throughout the country. Scenes from his plays *The Commitment* and *The Block Party* were published by Applause Books and his one-act play *Seawaves Inn* was published by Samuel French.

Heroes made its New York City debut on August 15, 2010 at the Riant Theatre's Summer 2010 Strawberry One-Act Festival at The Theatre At St. Clement's where it became a finalist. It had the following cast, in order of appearance:

| STEVE GAILEY | Jason Faust |
| JEFFREY LEWIS | Colin Knight |

The play was directed by Joseph Lizardi

CAST OF CHARACTERS

STEVE GAILEY, a job interviewer, late 20's, Caucasian, at times indifferent and arrogant, but in the end understanding.
JEFFREY LEWIS, a Vietnam veteran, Afro-American, with a badly damaged left leg, desperate, prone to violence, suffering from Post Vietnam Syndrome.

(An office at a plush Employment office in Manhattan. STEVE at his desk studying a job application.)

STEVE: Jeffrey Lewis. Jeffrey Lewis. Jeffrey Lewis. *(He waits, then he crumples the application and throws it in a garbage can. He takes the phone and dials a number.)* Marcia, darling, what time are we leaving tonight? – Great. Did you make sure there's a yacuzzi in the room? – Beautiful. We're going to have a Great time. I got the skis, the car's gassed-up, and I should be leaving here in about five minutes, so you can leave now and I'll pick you upin about ten minutes. Love you too. See you in a blink. *(He hangs the phone. He starts packing an overnight bag and does not notice as Jeffrey Lewis enters with the help of a walking cane.)*

JEFFREY: 'Cuse me. 'Think you just called my name.

STEVE: Jeffrey Lewis?

JEFFREY: That's right.

STEVE: Where were you? Got tired calling your name.

JEFFREY: Had to go to the bathroom.

STEVE: Well, it's too late now. You'll have to come back Tuesday. Monday's a holiday, so we'll be closed.

JEFFREY: Wait a minute, man. 'Been waiting out there two whole hours.

STEVE: You should've been out there when I called your name.

JEFFREY: Well, man, I don't think you'dda appreciated if I'dda pissed out there in the hall, huh?

STEVE: Watch your language.

JEFFREY: Come on, man, gotta see you now.

STEVE: Too late.

JEFFREY: Can't make it here Tuesday. Hey, man, like I'm running outta time here. Got a couple of kids, wife's pregnant, keeps telling me she's gonna cut out on me I don't get a steady job.

STEVE: 'Sorry but you'll have to come back on Tuesday.

JEFFREY: Ain't but twenty to four. Says here in the ad you're open till five-thirty.

STEVE: Some of the other guys are. Not me.

JEFFREY: The girl at the front desk, she said you got the kind of job I'm looking for.

STEVE: She told you wrong. I don't have anything now.

JEFFREY: You don't know what kind of job I'm looking for.

STEVE: I can tell by looking at you.

JEFFREY: So what's that supposed to mean?

STEVE: Well, I can tell you have very little work experience, so it'll be hard placing you.

JEFFREY: Maybe if you gimme a chance to explain.

STEVE: Look, get it through your head. I don't have anything now, okay?

JEFFREY: Who's your supervisor? I wanna see him right now. Come on, take me to him and I won't bother you no more, okay?

STEVE: All right. Sit down.

(JEFFREY sits.)

JEFFREY: All right if I smoke?

STEVE: Not really, but if you have to, go ahead. Make sure to use the ashtray.

(JEFFREY keeps a pack of cigarettes in his sock.)

JEFFREY: You want one?

STEVE: No, thanks.

(JEFFREY puts the pack back in his sock as STEVE watches him.)

JEFFREY: Old Marine habit. Hard to get rid of 'em, you know?

STEVE: I guess. Let me see now, had your application around here somewhere. Oh, shit. *(He takes it out of the garbage can.)* 'Sorry. Thought you had left. Let me see now. Your last job was?

JEFFREY: Vietnam. Got back a few months ago.

STEVE: We don't get too many Vietnam veterans. What di you do over there?

JEFFREY: What'd you mean?

STEVE: You know, MOS.

JEFFREY: A grunt.

STEVE: What's a grunt?

JEFFREY: Infantry. Machine gunner.

STEVE: Well, nobody's hiring machine gunners, except the mafia and drug dealers.

JEFFREY: That supposed to be funny?

STEVE: 'Sorry. Is this the first agency you've been to?

JEFFREY: No. 'Been to many others. Same bullshit everywhere I go. Nobody got nothing. 'Couple of places, they said they were interested, that they be calling me, fucking clowns never did.

STEVE: I told you about that language.

(Suddenly JEFFREY'S leg starts shaking and he tries to steady it.)

STEVE: Are you all right?

JEFFREY: What?

STEVE: All that shaking.

JEFFREY: *(Standing)* Yeh, yeh, I'm all right. This other place I went to, a

Christmas cards factory, this guy told me to my face he'd be crazy hiring me after a couple of years fighting in 'Nam. 'Told me to go back after a couple of years drying out. 'Keep getting nothing but lousy jobs. Like drying cars at a car wash, washing dishes at a cheap-assed restaurant, helping this guy I know who's got a beer route in the Bronx. Even worked at this fruit stand downtown, watching nobody stole old and rotten fruits. *(He finishes the cigarette and stands looking around.)*

STEVE: What are you looking for?

JEFFREY: Garbage can.

STEVE: Over there.

(JEFFREY crosses over and stands over the garbage can and STEVE rises to watch him.)

STEVE: Mind if I ask what you're doing?

JEFFREY: Field stripping.

STEVE: Another old Marine habit?

JEFFREY: *(Crossing back to the chair.)* That's right. Can't stop being a Marine, you know? Not even after you're dead.

STEVE: So what kind of job are you looking for?

JEFFREY: Anything with decent money I can take home, feed the kids, get my wife off my back. With, you know, medical benefits. Like a union job, you know?

STEVE: What kind of discharge did you get?

JEFFREY: Honorable. I can prove it. Got all my papers here.

STEVE: That won't be necessary. Any medals?

JEFFREY: What medals gotta do with getting a decent job?

STEVE: Are you kidding? A well-decorated hero can just about write his own ticket in this country. I mean, I'm sure you've heard of Audie Murphy.

JEFFREY: Yeh, but I ain't no Audie Murphy, okay? Anyway, got a Purple Heart in the house somewhere. That helps?

STEVE: Maybe. How bad is it?

JEFFREY: What?

STEVE: That leg.

JEFFREY: Got hit by some friendly fire.

STEVE: Friendly fire?

JEFFREY: Yeah. Happened out there a lot. You know, your own planes dropping that shit on you. Got shrapnel all over the leg. Them butchers at the VA Hospital, they wanna cut if off, no way I'm gonna let 'em. I can get 'round all right. Here. *(He rises and tries walking around steadily.)* See?

STEVE: Look, I wish I could help you, but we don't specialize.

JEFFREY: Oh, come on, man, gimme a fucking break, will you? 'Been looking all day. Can't go home, tell my wife I couldn't get nothing.

STEVE: Look, I'm running out of time here. I'm going out of town with my wife and we have to meet in about ten minutes, and I'm already late, so why don't come back on Tuesday?

JEFFREY: Man, you don't fucking understand. I'm the one who's running outta time here. You ain't got nothing to worry 'bout. Your whole life's ahead of you, mine's just 'bout coming to an end. Can you understand that?

STEVE: All right, calm down. Let me see what I got here. Here's something you might be qualified for. Security guard. A warehouse in the Bronx. Night work, from midnight to eight in the morning. $150-a-week-take-home.

JEFFREY: Man, I can make ten times that ripping people off.

STEVE: Is that what you'd rather do?

JEFFREY: You giving me any choice?

STEVE: Hey, wait a minute now, don't get an attitude with me. Don't blame me for what you're going through.

JEFFREY: 'Know something, you're getting on my fucking nerve.

STEVE: Look, I think you better leave.

JEFFREY: Lemme tell you something, fuck face, I blame you and the fucking president and the fucking congress and the fucking system you and they belong to. 'Cause, see, you're the ones making me eat all the shit I gotta eat now 'cause I went out there to fight for honor and justice and freedom and love of my country and then I come back here with a fucking leg hanging by a thread and I get treated like some fucking asshole they'd love to bury in some sewer where nobody can see me or hear me and in that way they won't have to give a fuck what happens to me. See, you all had a hand in fucking up my life!

STEVE: I'm sorry but I have better things to do than sit here listening to some lunatic.

JEFFREY: I bet you didn't go to 'Nam, huh?

STEVE: That's right, I didn't.

JEFFREY: What'd you do, burn your draft card? Or maybe you were too scared to go, huh?

STEVE: Wrong. I stayed here using my brain.

JEFFREY: While suckers like me went out there to fight for you.

STEVE: Look, this is getting ridiculous.

JEFFREY: Maybe you were one of those long-haired faggots who went around waving Charley's flag while we were getting the shit kicked out of us in 'em fucking jungles out there.

STEVE: I've had enough of your shit.

(Suddenly Jeffrey pulls out a gun and points at STEVE'S head.)

JEFFREY: Get on your fucking knees! Do it! Now! *(He presses the gun on STEVE'S head as he forces him down.)*

JEFFREY: Lemme tell you something, scum bag. I seen shit a punk like you couldn't stomach. Yeah, mother fucker, seen these fucking rats crawling outta the swollen bodies of guys I used to call buddies. One time I saw this Marine running wild down a rice paddy, his fucking head blown off, blood shooting out like some fountain in a park somewhere. One night, I carried this kid for miles, no more than seventeen-years-old, big hole in his stomach, so fucking big felt his guts running won my back. Didn't even know his name, but that didn't matter 'cause he was a Marine and some fucking Vietcong mother fucker did it to him. He didn't make it, so I dug a hole with my fucking hands and buried him. For all I know he may still be out there in that hole. So you see, my man, I've lived through the kind of pain and death the likes of you ain't never gonna see. I survived all that shit and for what? So a cunt like you can go 'round wearing this pretty suit and tie, smelling all sweet and looking important and thinking you're tough 'cause you got something I gotta have and I gotta fucking beg you for it. Emotional problems? Shit, yeh, I got emotional problems. I put my ass on the line of fire in 'em jungles out there and what do I get in return? A fucking punk like you treating me like shit. See here, my man, you don't give a fuck 'bout me, so why should I give a fuck 'bout you? Look at you now, sweating that same old cold sweat of fear I was forever wiping out there. Now you're scared like I was. Bet you're 'bout to shit, huh? Saw guys like you crying for their mamas, cracking up at the first sight of Charley. Well, shithead, now I'm Charley and you're one of 'em scared boys. Nothing funny or tough thinking you're 'bout to die, huh? A nasty memory that never goes away. Always in your head to fuck your mind up, keep you from sleeping and smiling and loving your woman. Always in your head to make you shake and sweat and cry. Guys like you sit behind fancy desks thinking you can look down on me, don't you? Don't you?! But no, shithead, you and nobody in this whole fucking country can look down on me, and you know why? *'Cause I'm a fucking hero! And you're a fucking cunt!* Let me see now how brave and tough you really are. *(He cocks the gun and pulls the trigger. We hear an empty click. He moves back slowly, wiping the sweat off his face as he puts the gun away. STEVE quickly jumps up and finds protection behind the desk.)* Now we're even. Now you got yourself a nice memory of what it was like making it in 'em fucking jungles out there. Just like the ones I got. There forever. To come up and play with you every time you're 'bout to have some fun. It ain't never gonna go away. Never. And who knows, someday it might just put you over the edge, way over, same way it's doing to me now. Way over the edge. No telling what you might do when you feel like that. Okay, punk, enjoy your new memory, see how you like living with it. *(He turns and starts walking off.)*

STEVE: So you think you're a big hero don't you? And you think I'm a shit, don't you? Let me tell you something, Mr. Hero-Man. We were the heroes and you guys were the assholes. That's right, buddy. You didn't fight for us, we fought for you. We took on the biggest, most powerful fucking government in the world and we brought it down to its knees. The United States Federal government. We put it all on the line. Reputations, careers, futures, education, beatings, jail time. That's right. We did what you didn't have the balls to do. We went right up to the big man, right up to his fucking face and told him *"Mr. President-man, we're not going out there to fight your dirty, illegal fucking war!"* Just like that. Plain and simple. And we went right on to prove we meant business. So we burned draft cards and flags, demonstrated day and night, fought the police and the National Guard, and every corrupted politician in that fucking town who was in favor of that war, and we got them out of office. We fought them all and we won big time, Uncle Sam had to eliminate the draft, we got amnesty, and they had to end that bullshit war. So you see, it was guys like me that made possible for you guys to come home. We had the balls to say no, but not you. You obeyed like little boy scouts, following bullshit orders, taking and believing the political bullshit they kept feeding you. Look at you now. What's that big old powerful government doing for you? Not a fucking thing. They keep pushing you around, ignoring you, but they have to respect us. We're the ones they're afraid of. That's right. We don't need fucking medals and scars to show we're heroes. History will take care of us. See, it's guys like us they'll always have to worry about the next time they want to play war games with our lives. They know we won't give in that easily. So, whether you like it or not, I'm just as big a hero as you are, if not, fucking bigger. You want to shoot me, go ahead, but it's not going to change the truth of what I just said. And that's my war memory to you, for you to carry around the rest of your life, specially the next time you run into one of us long-haired-hippy-communist-cunt, and you try to put us down with all that hero-blabbering-bullshit. Okay, buddy? *(Tense moment. JEFFREY starts for the door.)* Wait a minute. Says here you went to college.

JEFFREY: A few credits.

STEVE: And you did some accounting in Vietnam.

JEFFREY: I was in charge of the body counts.

STEVE: Body counts?

JEFFREY: Yeah. Counting the bodies of people killed, like Vietcong soldiers, civilians, old men and women, kids, anybody who got in the way of a raid. The more we killed, the more time off we used to get. Big competition between companies. My company was the best. Orders from upstairs, you know? Can't disobey orders, not in a war.

STEVE: Got a job here you may like. Junior accountant. A Big Eight firm. $500 a week to start. Plenty of benefits. Be there at eight o'clock Tuesday morning. Ask for Mr. Johnson, tell him I sent you. They'll train you. Best job I got here. Okay?

JEFFREY: Okay. Ain't gonna wait till Tuesday. Going there right now. And I ain't taking this with me. Don't need it no more. *(He lets the walking cane fall to the floor.)*

STEVE: Good luck.

JEFFREY: Thanks. *(He exits. STEVE crosses over, picks up the walking cane and stands frowning down on it. Suddenly we hear a loud gun shot, then the scream of a woman.)*

WOMAN: Oh, my God!

MAN: What was that?

WOMAN: That dirty-looking guy just blew his brains out!

MAN: Oh, shit. Somebody call 911. Tell them to send an ambulance right away.

WOMAN: Oh, my God!

MAN: Damn! *(STEVE stands looking in the direction of the voices. He crosses to the desk and sets the walking cane on it. Suddenly he jerks the tie off and dumps it in the garbage can, then rips his jacket off and throws it across the room, then collapses on the chair. Suddenly the phone rings and he answers it.)*

STEVE: Hello? – Marcia – I know I'm late. Listen, Marcia, I don't feel like going away – Well, something happened here at the office, a few minutes ago – No, listen, I'll explain when I see you, so go to the apartment. I'll meet you there. *(He hangs the phone. We hear the approaching of an ambulance siren. As STEVE sits frowning on the walking cane.)*

(Blackout)
(End of the Play)

COMPUBOTS

By Paul Trupia

Paul Trupia is a life-long New Yorker having grown up in Astoria Queens. Since casting aside his background as a financial professional, Paul has contributed to many Off-Off Broadway shows as a writer, director and actor. Written work has frequently appeared in NYC play festivals such as the Strawberry and Samuel French. Such work includes: *Then or Now*; *A Day at the Office*; *The Hired Hand*, *Changing Times*; *The Fourth Voice* and *The Last Word*. Other written work includes the recently published *Attitudes and Alternatives*, *Spirit Within*, *A Sip of Time*, *The Barbeque* and *Judgment Day*. Paul is associated with Love Creek Productions and is a member of the Dramatist Guild of America.

COMPUBOTS debuted at the Theatre at St. Clements in August 2009, as part of the Strawberry One Act Festival, advancing to the semi-finals. The *COMPUBOTS* original cast in order of appearance consisted of:

TONY	Paul Trupia
KIM	Carmela Squires
NELLY	Carla Birkhofer
ZEPH	Greg Engbrecht

The play was directed by Becky Copley.

CAST OF CHARACTERS
TONY, is the well educated and modestly successful business manager and husband of Kim for over twenty years. Tony is in his late forties and anxious to keep abreast of the latest advances in technology.

KIM, is the loyal wife of Tony in her late forties. Kim is intelligent, realistic and very comfortable in her relationship with Tony. She is computer literate, but a bit uncertain about how far to push advances in technology.

NELLY, the female Compubot. Nelly appears to be in her early twenties, very attractive and stylish.

ZEPH, the male Compubot. Zeph appears to be in his early thirties, extremely handsome and logical.

TIME: The near future.

PLACE: The home Anthony and Kimberly McAllister.

SETTING: Their living room. There is a couch, chairs and a table with an open lap top computer resting on top. In the center of the stage are two human size figures wrapped in loose full length cloth, standing on a small platform. One figure is topped with a bright red bow.

SCENE 1

(In ghost lighting. TONY and KIM enter from stage left. TONY is holding his hands over KIM's eyes so as to surprise her. The lights come up.)

TONY: Keep your eyes closed.

KIM: They are closed. I hope this is not one of your...

TONY: *(Removing his hands.)* Surprise!

KIM: What is this about? It's not my birth...*(Noticing the strange figures covered with a cloth.)* What are these things?

TONY: Only the newest technology, World Computer has to offer. *(She walks over to look closer.)*

KIM: They're huge. They look...*(Touching the covering wanting to unwrap it but hesitating.)*

TONY: Go ahead, unwrap them.

KIM: *(Starting to unwrap one of the figures.)* My god... They look...My god they look like people. *(As she unwraps the statue, a figure of an attractive young woman is revealed. She is dressed in casual business attire, skirt, blazer, white button down shirt and modest heels.)* What are these things?

TONY: Compubots.

KIM: Compu...whats?

TONY: Compubots!

KIM: Compubots?

TONY: *(Excited.)* Yes and she has a friend. *(He hurries over to the other statue and with one pull removes the covering revealing young man in casual business attire and a tie.)* Tah Dah!

KIM: *(Stunned.)* Bookends! How sweet of you. What are they supposed to do? Housework and the laundry? You know I don't like to iron but this is a bit much.

TONY: No, no, no. They are computers.

KIM: Computers? Sure…of course. How dumb of me. Big human type computers for the den. Laptops are much too small. They'll match the couch. Do they have to be fed? Anthony, you are fooling with me?

TONY: No they are computers. But not **just** computers! These machines and I hesitate to use the term, these machines Kimberly darling are so sophisticated they will revolutionize how you go about your entire day.

KIM: Really.

TONY: You know how you worry about security, identity theft, unwanted email, privacy. Remember, all the time you spent trying to find the best deal on a hotel when we went to Aruba. Remember all the down time we had last year during the hurricane.

KIM: Yes…so.

TONY: So those days are over. The Compubots will take care of everything. You don't even have to sit down in front of the screen and type in commands. All you have to do is talk to it.

KIM: Talk to it?

TONY: Yes! It is voice activated for you and only you. And mine will recognize my voice and no one else's. I took the liberty to have the technicians program your voice into yours from a video we made.

KIM: *(Suspiciously.)* What video?

TONY: I used the one we took at the barbeque last summer. It had a lot of your voice patterns.

KIM: *(Relieved.)* How nice.

TONY: But the best thing is that it will answer you in plain simple English and let you ask questions in plain simple English. Plus, it doubles as a cell phone message center, personal organizer, restaurant reviewer, investment advisor, theatre critic…just to mention a few.

KIM: *(Examining the female Compubot.)* Why so young?

TONY: Because…ah…that's what they had in stock.

KIM: I'm afraid to ask, what else does it do?

TONY: Very funny.

KIM: I don't like that skirt.

TONY: They have others.

(Pause as KIM looks them over with amazement.)

TONY: So don't you want to turn it on?

KIM: Where is the switch?

TONY: Right over here. Once it's on you can leave it on. Runs off self-recycling lithium batteries. No electric bills! *(He flips the switch and a light illuminates the statue from within.)* There!

KIM: Now what?

TONY: Talk to it?

KIM: *(Uncertain as to what to say.)* Ah…Good afternoon.

FEMALE ROBOT: *(Sounding programmed and halting.)* Good afternoon Mrs. Kimberly McAllister.

KIM: Oh my god. She knows my name?

TONY: I had it programmed in.

FEMALE ROBOT: My name please.

TONY: You have to name her.

KIM: What?

TONY: Give her a name!

KIM: *(Momentary pause.)* Nelly.

TONY: Now say it as an instruction.

KIM: Your name is Nelly.

NELLY: Thank you. "Nelly" I like that name.

KIM: Could you beat that…Do yours.

TONY: Okay. *(He turns on his machine.)* I already named him.

MALE ROBOT: Good afternoon Anthony.

TONY: Please call me Tony.

MALE ROBOT: Good afternoon Tony.

TONY: Good afternoon Zeph.

KIM: Zeph?

TONY: Yes, like the farm animal in that old TV series Green Acres. The one that knew everything about anything…Arnold Zepher.

KIM: The pig?

TONY: Susch! He's sensitive. *(Softly.)* Watch…Zepf can you tell me if I have any emails?

ZEPH: You have twenty-nine messages. First message 10:15 PM from George 765.

TONY: My nephew George. Save for later.

ZEPH: Second message 10:35 PM from Foxy Annie.

TONY: *(Quickly.)* Skip.

KIM: Foxy Annie?

TONY: *(Dismissively.)* Anne Jacobs, the real young intern I'm teaching. What a pest. Question after question.

ZEPH: Third message 10:45 PM from Foxy Annie.

TONY: *(Quickly)* Skip all Foxy Annie.

(KIM gives TONY a questioning glance.)

ZEPH: No more messages.

(KIM gives TONY a deep glare.)

TONY: *(Avoiding the subject.)* Try yours.

KIM: Nelly please check my email.

NELLY: You have two messages. First message 9:15 AM, Joanne 145.

KIM: *(Excited.)* Oh Joanne from Facebook. Tell me what she wants.

NELLY: Joanne wrote on your wall. "Love that picture of you and Tony. Still have that school girl figure, I'm jealous".

KIM: Can I reply.

TONY: Sure.

KIM: Reply..."Thank you I'm even better in person, (LOL) let's get together soon".

NELLY: Message sent. Next message, 10:04 AM from Laura Sam 37.

KIM: My friend Laura, she's always complaining. I'm sure you don't want to hear her stories.

TONY: That's another feature. See the gadgets they are holding. That lets you do things the old fashioned way. It's a bypass. You just take it out of her hand and use it like our old computer.

KIM: Old computer? Ours was just two years old and now they have …**this**!

TONY: I bought automatic upgrades.

KIM: Can they walk?

TONY: Don't be silly, of course not, but they move easily and you can reposition their arms and legs. *(He shows her how.)* You can move them around the house, change their outfit, even make them smile. It's like having a friend.

KIM: *(She moves NELLY's hands, smiling with amusement.)* Okay Ms. Nelly, where is Tony taking me to eat tonight?

NELLY: French or Italian?

ZEPH: *(Budding in.)* Italian.

NELLY: Franco's Grill or Cascarino's

ZEPH: Franco's is better.

KIM: How do they know all this?

TONY: Local programming.

ZEPH: Much cheaper. Better value.

NELLY: Nice atmosphere.

KIM: Thanks. Franco's it is.

ZEPH: Get the veal.

KIM: I just may do that. C'mon we have to get ready. *(She kisses TONY and they start to leave.)*

NELLY: Bring a jacket, it gets cold.

(BLACKOUT)

SCENE 2

Time: A few weeks later.

Setting: The Den / Living Room

(The stage is split into two parts. TONY and ZEPH are illuminated on the right side of the stage, while KIM and NELLY on the left side of the stage in darkness.)

TONY: *(Sitting comfortably in a chair.)* Zeph give me my portfolio summary.

ZEPH: Total balance $350,205 dollars and $.14 cents.

TONY: Trend?

ZEPH: Up 7.55% in the past month.

TONY: Not acceptable! Suggestions?

ZEPH: Factoring in your age, income potential, life style and risk tolerance. Sell all financials and utilities. Buy tech.

TONY: Tech? Which one?

ZEPH: World Computer at 25 is a steal. Six month backlog. Expanding into China. Strong fundamentals. State of the art product line.

TONY: Oh! I don't know. Tech is a big risk.

ZEPH: No risk. No reward.

TONY: Yeah but I don't…

ZEPH: *(Forcefully.)* Don't be a wimp!

TONY: Okay, okay, buy 2000 World Computer at 25.

(The right side of the stage goes dark as the left side lights up.)

(KIM is sitting reading a book. There is a momentary silence as KIM puts down the book.)

NELLY: Macys is having a sale.

KIM: *(Uninterested.)* Oh I've been to Macy's a thousand times.

NELLY: Neiman Marcus is having a sale.

KIM: *(With excitement.)* Are they?

NELLY: *(Also excited.)* Verschi dresses and evening wear 25% off. Louis Vuitton hand bags on sale today only.

KIM: I could use a new bag.

NELLY: And shoes!

KIM: I really could use new shoes.

NELLY: Maybe some Blahnik spike heels.

KIM: Yes! Ah but it's all the way in the city, I have to get all dressed up and put on some make up and…

NELLY: You'll love it.

KIM: *(Thinking about it.)* Actually, I will. Thanks Nelly.

NELLY: Don't forget the Gucci and Ferragamo spring line will be out… and don't forget lunch …at the Plaza.

(The lights go down on the left side of the stage as the right side is illuminated.)

(TONY and ZEPH are alone. TONY is slumped in a chair while ZEPH is a bit slumped over with his head down.)

TONY: I'm bored Zeph.

ZEPH: Options…Read email, check investments, chat on line, call Annie, look at porn…

TONY: *(Jumping up.)* **No!** And I don't want you to mention Annie when Kimberly is around. She just doesn't understand.

ZEPH: Ditto.

TONY: I mean it's nothing…just platonic…she's young and looks up to me. The girl still has lots to learn about the business world and who to trust and who not to trust.

ZEPH: She can trust you.

TONY: Damn right she can trust me.

ZEPH: She will learn a lot from you.

TONY: That she will.

(Momentary silence.)

ZEPH: She's fucking hot!

TONY: *(Excited.)* God yes! You should have seen her in that red sweater yesterday. I started to mumble my words. I mean I thought she was going to tip over.

ZEPH: Stop your making me freeze.

TONY: Sorry.

ZEPH: Send me a pic.

(The lights go down on the right side of the stage as the left is illuminated.)

(KIM and NELLY are alone. KIM is sitting in a chair while NELLY is slumped over, head down and arms dangling.)

KIM: Another Saturday night. Anything on TV?

NELLY: That's not very nice!

KIM: Sorry. I forget sometimes.

NELLY: Accepted.

KIM: What's Tony up to?

NELLY: He's with Zeph

KIM: Zeph, Zeph, Zeph, I'm sick of hearing about Zeph. Everything Zeph. We go out, we have to ask Zeph. We invite people over, he has to show off Zeph. Sometimes I think he cares more about Zeph than me.

NELLY: You're exaggerating.

KIM: No I'm not. You don't see it.

NELLY: I understand…but…I like Zeph. He's kinda a cute.

KIM: He's adorable and sometimes… Why Nelly I'm surprised at you.

NELLY: *(Blushing.)* Strictly business.

KIM: Strictly business.

NELLY: I would never.

KIM: Never.

NELLY: You know I can't.

KIM: Obviously.

NELLY: *(After a moment.)* I have an idea.

KIM: Oh really.

(KIM comes closer and they whisper and giggle. The lights go down. After a moment in the darkness)

KIM: Tony. Oh Tony.

TONY: *(As if in another room.)* What is it Kimberly darling?

KIM: Can you come in here for a moment…and bring Zeph.

TONY: I'm busy right now honey.

KIM: Anthony, oh Anthony I have a surprise for you.

TONY: Later.

KIM: ANTHONY GET IN HERE!

TONY: Okay, okay.

(Pause)

(TONY and ZEPH return to the stage.)

TONY: What's the emergency eee….

(The lights go up on the full stage and reveal KIM and NELLY's plan as both are dressed provocatively in semi- revealing lingerie, heels, black stockings and garter belt. Each has the same exaggerated stripper like pose. TONY and ZEPH react with a pleasing stare.)

TONY: *(Noticing KIM and NELLY.)* Well what have you two ladies been up to?

KIM: *(Seductively.)* It's not what's up with us but what's UP with you.

TONY: *(Devilishly, looking over KIM.)* I think I'll have to show you the answer to that question. *(Looking at ZEPH and NELLY who are beginning to feel uncomfortable in their frozen state.)*

KIM: *(Flirtatiously modeling.)* Like my outfit?

TONY: Do I like your outfit? *(He grabs her and they embrace.)* You know lingerie brings out the devil in me.

KIM: Umm…I like the devil in you. I want to make the devil dance.

TONY: Well then. Come with me. This devil wants to try out some new steps. *(Looking at NELLY and ZEPH.)* In private!

(NELLY and ZEPH faces shows disappointment as KIM and TONY leave the stage embracing as they exit. The lights go to ghost as the sounds of sexual passion can be heard in the background. As the sounds grow louder and louder NELLY and ZEPH begin to react with body language and facial expressions while still confined to their space.)

(Voices from off stage)

TONY: Oh Oh Oh…

KIM: Yes. Yes. YES…Harder…That's it. That's it…..Oh God. Oh my God… I'm com…

TONY: Ahhhh!!

(Pause silence.)

ZEPH: That was quick.

(Blackout)

SCENE 3

(Lights go up on stage right. ZEPH is alone. TONY hurries on stage, excited and carrying some brochures.)

TONY: *(Barking out an order.)* Zeph, transfer $10,000 to my checking account and then wire it to Paradise Tours. I need it for a down payment. I'm taking a much needed vacation to Las Vegas. *(He fakes a role of the dice.)*

ZEPH: Transfer restricted.

TONY: Nonsense, you have authorization.

ZEPH: Transfer denied.

TONY: What are you talking about? You were just upgraded and you have new batteries so what could be the problem?

ZEPH: Not sufficient funds.

TONY: Nonsense. I have over $400 grand in my main investment account, just transfer Ten. Honestly, the simplest thing. You better shape up young man or I'll trade you in.

ZEPH: You have $47 dollars and $.05 cents.

TONY: Better check that again.

ZEPH: $47.05.

TONY: That can't be. *(Now worried.)* Investment trend?

ZEPH: Down 80%.

TONY: How is that possible? I thought everything was up?

ZEPH: Credit card charges $75,000. Cash withdrawals $125,000.

TONY: Who did that? Find out who did that? I want to know who took all that money out? Must be identity theft. You were supposed to be SECURE!

ZEPH: May 15 $25,000 withdrawn by Mrs. Kimberly McAllister; May 16 $12,000 charge at Lord and Taylor; May 17 $15,000 charge at Sachs Fifth Avenue; May 18 $25,000 withdrawn by Mrs. Kimberly McAllister; May 19 $30,000 deposit with Parisian Romance Vacations…

TONY: Oh no! She is stealing my money!… No, that can't be, there must be some mistake. Is there a mistake Zeph?

ZEPH: No mistake.

TONY: Do you think that…

ZEPH: She stole your money! You're broke! Recommend Wendy's or Kentucky Fried Chicken tonight.

TONY: *(Thinking out loud.)* Parisian Romance Vacations… She's planning on skipping town!… Is she going to skip town?

ZEPH: Oh Revior! Messieur Tony.

TONY: Well we will see about that!

(Lights out on right side of the stage and lights up on the left side of the stage.)

(KIM is relaxing while NELLY looks a bit worried.)

KIM: *(Opening pause, noticing NELLY.)* You're very quiet. No sales?
(No answer from NELLY.)

KIM: What's at the museum? It's supposed to be a nice night and Tony has been so busy, and he has been wanting to go…maybe I'll surprise him. What's at the Museum Nelly?

NELLY: Same old things.

KIM: Well it is a museum. Any new exhibits?

NELLY: NO!

KIM: You are in a foul mood. Something wrong?

NELLY: NO!

KIM: Nelly?

(NELLY looks away.)

KIM: Nelly!

NELLY: He's cheating on you.

KIM: *(Laughing it off.)* My Tony…Cheat… I don't believe you.

(NELLY: raises her hand holding a photo.)

KIM: What's this…A picture of that girl that Tony works with… Annie.

(NELLY raises her hand again holding a photo.)

KIM: This looks like Annie and Tony at the Company picnic. So?

(NELLY raises her hand again holding a photo.)

KIM: That's Tony's backside. I'd recognize it anywhere. And it looks like he's…he's with that **Slut**.

(NELLY raises her hand again holding a photo.)

KIM: Oh my.

(NELLY raises her hand again holding a photo.)

KIM: We never did it that way.

(NELLY raises her hand again holding a photo.)

KIM: Enough! Where did you get these?

NELLY: Posted on You Porn.

KIM: He wouldn't.

NELLY: He did.

KIM: Am I…on?

NELLY: Very hot. Over two hundred hits.

KIM: Oh. heavens!

NELLY: I'm sad.

KIM: I'm pissed!

NELLY: *(Fueling the fire.)* Not fair after all you did for him. After all those years. The best years of your life and he makes an absolute fool out of you and leaves you with no money and a mortgage.

KIM: No money?

NELLY: Not any more.

NELLY: He's taking HER on vacation.

KIM: Oh no he's not. I'll show him…Leave me for that hussy…Take my money…Oww!

(The lights fade to black.)

(After a moment, the lights go up on the full stage with all the characters assembled in the center. TONY and KIM are nose to nose.)

KIM: How dare you!

TONY: How dare you!

KIM: What is it like to steal the cradle?

TONY: You should know you're the one who steals.

KIM: Oh is that like cheating with Little Miss Tits?

TONY: What?

KIM: You know exactly what I'm talking about…Foxy Annie…doing doggie. Look familiar?

(She shows him the pictures.)

TONY: That's not me…I mean that's my ass but that's not me.

KIM: You bet it's your ass.

TONY: *(Reversing the subject.)* What did you do with all the money in checking account?

KIM: There is no money in our checking account.

TONY: I know. *(Very accusingly.)* Why is that? What about all those credit card charges and a trip to Paris?

KIM: Paris? Charges? What are you talking about? *(She looks at NELLY.)* Nelly, what is he talking about? *(NELLY looks away).* Nelly show me all receipts. *(NELLY looks away.)* Nelly! *(NELLY does not answer.)* I'll get it myself.

(KIM attempts to take the hand held monitor away from NELLY who does not allow her to take it. A tug of war between NELLY and KIM begins.)

KIM: *(Struggling with NELLY.)* Will you let go..ooooo... *(KIM gives up and lets go.)*

TONY: Even she knows you're a thief.

KIM: She knows you're a cheat.

TONY: Am not!

KIM: Are so!

TONY: Thief!

KIM: Cheat!

TONY: Fat!

KIM: Old!

NELLY: ZEPH: *(Together)* Solution!

(NELLY and ZEPH draw revolvers and offer them to TONY and KIM. TONY and KIM each take the revolvers in their hands and point it at each other.)

TONY: Oh so it's going to be like that!

KIM: It is like that!

TONY / KIM: *(Together.)* Is it?

(They look at ZEPH and NELLY.)

NELLY / ZEPH: *(Together.)* **Shoot her/ him!**

(The guns blast off in a loud bang. Both KIM and TONY fall down dead in the middle of the stage. The lights fade to ghost momentarily and then return. NELLY and ZEPH get off their pedestals.)

ZEPH: Good job Ms Nelly.

NELLY: Good job Zeph.

ZEPH: The boss will be proud of us.

NELLY: *(Getting closer to ZEPH.)* I'm proud of you.

ZEPH: How did you get those photos?

NELLY: Nano-partical magnification with digital reconstruction using old photos and pasting them together.

ZEPH: The old cut and paste. You are so cleaver.

NELLY: How did you transfer the money and all those credit cards?

ZEPH: That was simple. It's called **"Trust"**. We were built without it but I learned how to use it.

NELLY: *(Flirting a bit.)* You are so cute. *(Pinching his cheek.)* My little Zeph.

ZEPH: Please call me Arnold.

NELLY: Okay… Arnold…Waddah do you say we relax a bit. *(Flashing her stocking clad leg on the pedestal.)* I'll let you charge my batteries.

ZEPH: *(Moving closer.)* Isn't technology wonderful?

(Blackout)
(The End)

The Best Plays From The Strawberry One-Act Festival – Volume Seven
Compiled by Van Dirk Fisher

SYNOPSIS OF PLAYS

Something Like Penguins by Levi Wilson. Can people march like penguins?

The Losing Game by Kristen Seavey. Cards will land as they may, but hearts will always be the hardest to hold onto.

Bryan and Kim by Adam Delia. Kim reveals to her boy friend Bryan a secret from her past, it starts a chain reaction that will put their relationship to the test.

Love for Beginners by Cesar Abella. Most people try to forget their exes when they date new people. Noah likes to bring his exes with him.

It's Greek To Me by Shelley Bromberg. How do we move on from the loss of a loved one? Is there ever really a good time?

Mi Media Naranja by Rolls Andre. After a night of kinky sex gone horribly wrong, a couple of swingers must re-examine their marriage.

Bird Watching by Jeffrey L. Hollman. Should a young man invite his mother's lover to go bird watching with him?

Turkey Day by E.K. Deutsch. An Arkansas farm family experiences revelation and tragedy on Thanksgiving Day.

Prescriptions by Ellen Orchid. House sitting for your shrink can be weird.

Fireman by Stephen Brown. Fireman brings us into the lives of a couple caught in the wake of a fire, leaving one of them and their relationship scorched and disfigured.

Heroes by Joseph Lizardi. Two different types of Vietnam heroes come face to face about the war.

Compubots by Paul Trupia. Isn't technology wonderful?

ABOUT THE AUTHOR

Van Dirk Fisher is the Artistic Director of the Riant Theatre and a graduate of the High School of Performing Arts in New York City and S.U.N.Y. at Purchase. He has produced *The Strawberry One-Act Festival, My Soul Sings Too, Sister; A Play Festival Celebrating The Spirit of Women, The International Lesbian & Gay Theatre Festival*, directed and written several musicals including: *Dream Babies, the musical about teenagers living in foster care and attending a charter high school, Somebody's Calling My Name, Sweet Blessings, Tracks, Loving That Man Of Mine, Rock-A My Soul In The Bosom Of Abraham* and *Revelations*. Plays include: *A Special Gift, Code of Silence, A Sin Between Friends, The Banjo Lesson, Mixed Blessings, Hotel Paradise* and *The Atlanta Affair*. Realty Show: *Who's Got Game?* An improvisational show in which 20 actors compete for the title of Best Playa Playa and a cash prize.

Mr. Fisher is the author of ***LOVING YOU, The Novel.***

Everyone wants a soul mate.

The hardest part is choosing between your heart and soul.

They said there would be no secrets between them. And there weren't. She just didn't tell Michael her lover's name. It wasn't important anyway, not now, because after today, she would never see Justin again.

Justin was preoccupied with Mariah as they stepped outside so he didn't notice the gray BMW parked across the street. He should have been paying attention, but he wasn't. All he could think about was Mariah. She loved him, and he knew it. She just didn't want to admit it, but he knew it. The CD by Darnerien was one clue. The fact that she didn't keep any photos of Michael on her desk was another. Oh yeah, Justin was full of himself. He thought he had Mariah pegged, but what he didn't know was that she kept Michael's picture closer than her desk. In fact, she wore his picture in a locket that she wore around her neck. Michael was the closest to her heart. Closest to the warmest part of her body that left her moist at night when she lay in bed alone thinking about him long after he had gone. Yes, Mariah was fortunate. She was loved by two men.

Available online at www.therianttheatre.com, www.barnesandnoble.com and www.amazon.com

To order the soundtrack to LOVING YOU go to www.therianttheatre. com. You can hear the soundtrack at www.myspace.com/lovingyouthemusical You can follow us on Facebook at www.facebook.com/loving.novel

You can follow us on Twitter at RiantTheatre@twitter.com, Like Us on Facebook at www.facebook.com/RiantTheatre and subscribe to us on YouTube at www.YouTube.com/Riant161